Measurement

LEONIE ~~~

Teacher Timesavers

Published by Scholastic Ltd,
Villiers House,
Clarendon Avenue,
Leamington Spa,
Warwickshire CV32 5PR

© 1996 Scholastic Ltd
Text © 1996 Leonie McKinnon

123456789   6789012345

Author Leonie McKinnon
Editor Gill Munton
Series designer Joy White
Designer Toby Long
Illustrations Caroline Ewen
Cover illustration Frances Lloyd
Cover photograph Martyn Chillmaid

Designed using Aldus Pagemaker
Processed by Pages Bureau, Leamington Spa
Printed in Great Britain by Clays Ltd, Bungay, Suffolk

British Library Cataloguing-in-Publication Data
A catalogue record for this book is
available from the British Library.

ISBN 0-590-53458-0

All rights reserved. This book is sold subject to the condition that it shall not, by way of trade or otherwise, be lent, hired out or otherwise circulated without the publisher's prior consent in any form of binding or cover other than that in which it is published and without a similar condition, including this condition, being imposed upon the subsequent purchaser.

The right of Leonie McKinnon to be identified as the Author of this Work has been asserted by her in accordance with the Copyright, Designs and Patents Act 1988.

No part of this publication may be reproduced, stored in a retrieval system, or transmitted, in any form or by any means, electronic, mechanical, photocopying, recording or otherwise, without the prior permission of the publisher. This book remains copyright, although permission is granted to copy pages 13 to 144 for classroom distribution and use only in the school which has purchased the book, or by the teacher who has purchased this book and in accordance with the CLA licensing agreement. Photocopying permission is given for purchasers only and not for borrowers of books from any lending service.

Contents

Teachers' Notes   5

Length
Caterpillars	13
As long as	14
Me	15
Aliens	16
Paperclips	17
What shall I use?	18
Measuring with hands and feet	19
A metre	20
Snails	21
Round and round	22
Make a metre	23
The estimating game	24
Jumps	25
A long journey	26
How far?	27
Sports	28
Millimetres	29
Dinosaur fun	30
Scale	31
Scale drawing	32
Miles to kilometres	33

Mass
Heavier or lighter?	34
Using a balance	35
Which is heavier?	36
Seesaw	37
Blocks	38
My shoe	39
Plasticine	40
Changing shape	41
Kilograms	42
Predicting	43
Smaller weights	44
Grams	45
Gifts	46
Find the weight	47
Tins and packets	48
Grams, kilograms or tonnes?	49
Throw the ball	50
Estimating more than one	51
Weighing ourselves	52
Muffins	53
Wet and dry	54
Net weight/gross weight	55

Capacity and volume
Full or empty?	56
Half-full	57
Which holds most?	58
Cupfuls	59
How many?	60
New paint	61
Litres	62
Make a litre	63
More or less?	64
Halves and quarters	65
Spoons	66
Evaporation	67
Reading a scale 1	68
Reading a scale 2	69
Litres and millilitres	70
Cooking	71
Pints and gallons	72
Volume problems (cards)	73
Boxes	74
Lids	75
In the shops	76
Cubes	77
Cubes and cuboids	78
Capacity and volume	79

Time
Night and day	80
After school	81
O'clock	82
Days of the week	83
Making clocks	84

The seasons	85
The calendar 1	86
The calendar 2	87
Birthdays	88
Timing devices	89
Telling the time	90
On time	91
TV times	92
In a minute	93
Matching	94
Writing the date	95
Morning and afternoon	96
Seconds	97
24-hour clocks	98
Tickets	99
Triathlon times	100
Babysitting	101
Speed	102

Perimeter

How far round?	103
Measuring perimeters	104
Solve the riddle	105
Borders	106
Squares	107
Rectangles	108
Christmas lights	109
Swimming pools	110
Squared paper	111
Regular polygons	112
Different shapes	113
On the farm	114
Doubling up	115
Lakes	116
Perimeter problems (cards)	117
Find the perimeter	118
Joining shapes	119
Athletics	120
Warm-up	121
Circles	122

Area

Large and small	123
Larger or smaller?	124
Measuring with blocks	125
Measuring with books	126
Measuring with newspaper	127
Geoboards	128
Alphabet area	129
Hands	130
Leaves	131
Square centimetres	132
Find the area	133
Square metres	134
Designing a garden	135
Blackout!	136
Squares	137
Rectangles	138
Gardens	139
Right-angled triangles	140
One into two	141
Kites	142
New carpets	143
Measuring farmland	144

Introduction

Measurement is one of the most practical and useful areas of mathematics. When children first come to school, they can probably already make direct comparisons between objects of different sizes and use much of the language associated with measurement. We should build on these early experiences, initially through measurement activities in non-standard units. As the need for accuracy becomes apparent, standard units should be introduced.

Measuring skills have applications throughout the primary Mathematics curriculum. This book provides a range of ready-to-use materials which help children to develop these skills. The activities are suitable for children of differing abilities, and may be used on their own or to supplement any scheme of work. Some initial discussion and teaching will usually be necessary, especially if a concept is being encountered for the first time. It is up to the teacher's professional judgement as to which activities are suitable for a particular child at a particular stage.

The activities may be used to introduce an idea, for consolidation, for extension work, for homework, for assessment or as revision. Most are of a practical nature and will lend themselves to independent, pair or group work. Children should also be encouraged to solve the real measuring problems which arise naturally in the classroom. These may be in any curriculum area but are especially common in Science, Art, PE and Technology. Children will also produce their own questions and ideas which may stimulate work on measurement.

It helps children's understanding if they can communicate their ideas verbally. Discussing mathematical concepts helps them to consolidate knowledge, to learn different ways of thinking and to clarify their thoughts. The language associated with measurement is extremely important and children should be given every opportunity to develop their vocabulary. The activities in this book place emphasis on the skill of estimating, and children should be encouraged to justify their ideas through discussion. Wherever possible, there should be follow-up discussion between children or between children and teacher.

Most of the equipment required for the activities will be readily available in school. Children should be encouraged to select appropriate equipment and to use it accurately.

About the author

Leonie McKinnon trained as a primary school teacher in Australia. She has several years' teaching experience in Australia, the Middle East, Britain, Singapore and the Netherlands.

Using this book

The content of this book closely follows the requirements of all the UK curriculum documents for Mathematics. The activities are arranged in six chapters: Length, Mass, Capacity and volume, Time, Perimeter and Area. Within each chapter the activity sheets are arranged in ascending order of difficulty. Answers are provided in the teachers' notes where appropriate, and ❏ indicates extension work.

Length

Caterpillars Introduce this activity by asking the children to match pairs of ribbons or strips of paper that are the same length.
❏ Ask the children to cut out the pairs of

Teachers' Notes

caterpillars and put them in order from longest to shortest.

As long as This activity explores the direct comparison of objects of different lengths.
❏ More activities based on the term 'as tall as' could be attempted. For example, children could make a tower 'as tall as' themselves.

Me This activity asks the children to compare their height with that of various objects.
❏ The children could add a sentence to go with each picture. For example: 'A giraffe is taller than me.'

Aliens As an introduction to this activity, ask the children to put groups of their friends in order from tallest to shortest.

Paperclips This activity explores the use of a chain of paperclips as a non-standard unit of measurement. As an alternative you could use ten Multilink or Unifix cubes, or straws on a string.

What shall I use? Some previous experience of measuring with non-standard units will be necessary before the children look at how units of different sizes may be used for measuring different objects.

Measuring with hands and feet Early units of measurement were based on parts of the human body. For example, the cubit was an ancient unit of length approximately equal to the length of a forearm, and a palm was the width of four fingers. These units were convenient as they were always available and easy to use. However, they were not accurate as people differ in size.
❏ Encourage the children to use a body part of their choice to make a measuring strip.

A metre This activity explores 1m as a standard unit of measurement.
❑ Try using ¼m, ¾m or a decimetre (dm) as a standard unit.

Snails This activity asks children to measure distances which are not single straight lines.
Answers: 1st Bill, 2nd Paul, 3rd John, 4th Boris.
❑ Let the children draw some more trails for someone else to measure.

Round and round Prepare for this activity by making a list of suitable cylindrical objects.
❑ Instead of string the children could use a strip of paper, or they could mark the object, roll it for one complete revolution and measure the distance covered. Cardboard or paper cylinders could be cut open, flattened out and measured.

Make a metre This game can be adapted for any length, for example ¼m, ½m or ¾m.

The estimating game Make sure that the players are very clear about what is being measured and which units will be used.
❑ Later, the children could add their own cards to the game.

Jumps
❑ This activity could lead on to other investigations. For example, does the person with the longest arm have the longest throw?

A long journey This game involves converting between centimetres, metres and kilometres. The children could convert everything to the same unit.

How far? Introduce this activity by taking the children on a 1km walk so that they gain an understanding of how far 1km is.
Answers: 62km, 29km, 72km or 84km, 100km, 123km, 122km.
❑ Offer the children local maps and work out a cycle route for a distance of 100km. Explore the ways in which this route could be used for a race of 200km.

Sports This activity uses measuring for a practical purpose.
❑ The children could explore the possibilities of overlapping some of the courts to save space.

Millimetres This activity explores the millimetre as a standard unit of measurement.
Answers: 300mm, 250mm, 120mm, 40mm, 5mm, 360mm, 180mm, 50mm 1350mm, 4500mm.

Dinosaur fun This activity asks children to measure the distance between two points on a map, and use a scale to work out the actual distance (1cm = 1km).
Answers: 12km, 8km, 13km, 8km, 7km.

Scale This activity relates well to map reading. Try to give the children experience of as many different maps/scales as possible.
Answers: 48km, 120km, 120km, 80km, 144km, 6 hours, 400km.

Scale drawing
❑ The children could make a scale drawing of the classroom and use this information to try various arrangements of the furniture without picking up a single chair. Discuss the advantages of this.

Miles to kilometres
Answers: Dargo 6km, Staris 1736km, Blimpy 20km, Watcha 902km, Gympie 589km, Lowen 122km, Dorsal 53km, Radit 208km, Garner 411km, Geeves 1152km.
❑ The children could also convert from kilometres back to miles which is a particularly useful skill when travelling to continental Europe.

Mass

The terms 'weight' and 'mass' are commonly used to mean the same thing. On a technical level, however, they mean different things. Mass is the quantity of matter a physical body contains, whereas weight is the force experienced by a body as the result of gravitational pull. At the primary school level there should be no great difficulties if both terms are used. 'Weight' is the one more often encountered in everyday life.

Heavier or lighter? This activity asks the children to compare their weight with that of other people and objects, and to use the terms 'heavier' and 'lighter'.

Using a balance Objects that can easily be handled by the children are most suitable for this activity.

Which is heavier? You will need to collect the objects shown on the activity sheet beforehand.

Seesaw Activities involving 'body maths' require a sensitive approach.
❑ Do the members of each group weigh more in total than the teacher? If safety permits, try it!

Blocks This activity uses blocks as a non-standard unit of measurement. Discuss the fact that an estimate does not have to be accurate and consider the 'reasonableness' of answers.

My shoe The children are not necessarily trying to balance items one for one, and may need to be encouraged to use several marbles, shells or cups of sand.

Plasticine Begin this activity with a demonstration if the children have not used non-standard units before.

Changing shape This activity demonstrates conservation of mass. Emphasise to the children that they must continue to use the same lump of Plasticine. It is only the shape that changes.

Kilograms This activity introduces 1kg as a standard unit of measurement. Discuss with the children how they made their ½kg bags of sand.

Compare the different methods they used.
Predicting Emphasise that a 'level cup' should be used. Try balancing a heaped cup with a less than full cup to demonstrate the discrepancies that would otherwise occur.
Smaller weights This activity uses grams as a standard unit of measurement.
❏ Keep the weighed quantities in small plastic bags and use them to make a display.
Grams This activity ask children to weigh in grams and then to convert from grams to kilograms. Tell the children to pick up each object to help them to estimate its weight in grams.
Gifts Have a few real packages available for the children to investigate first. They could weigh them and record the weights using the method shown on the worksheet.
Find the weight This activity asks children to add lists of weights in grams and convert them into kilograms if appropriate.
Answers: 200g, 550g, 810g, 905g, 560g, 1.03kg, 1.24kg.
Tins and packets This activity explores the idea that weight is not always related to size.
Grams, kilograms or tonnes? Make sure the children have had plenty of practical experience of selecting appropriate measuring devices and units before attempting this activity.
Throw the ball You may have to change the list of balls according to which balls are available. Be aware of the safety implications of this activity, especially when using the shot.
Estimating more than one This activity is easier if the children already know how to multiply by 10.
Weighing ourselves Weighing children in another class is less personal. Depersonalise the results even further by giving each child to be weighed a number so no names are recorded.

You may need to explain to the children that the average weight is calculated by dividing the total weight by the number of children weighed.
Muffins Children need to be able to use those Imperial measures which are still in everyday use, for example, pints, ounces and miles.
Answers: 150g, 40g, 50g, 110ml, 110g, 50g, 110g, 25g, 75g.
❏ Other recipes could be used, with conversions from metric to Imperial measures. Discuss the implications of using two measuring systems.
Wet and dry This activity works well as part of a Science unit of study on 'Materials and their properties'.
Net weight/gross weight This activity explores the terms 'net weight' and 'gross weight'.
❏ Each child could choose a packaged product and explore its net/gross weight. Which weight is advertised? Is this fair?

Capacity and volume

The term 'volume' refers to the amount of space inside a solid figure. Volume is generally measured in cubic centimetres (cm^3) or cubic metres (m^3). The term 'capacity' relates directly to the concept of volume but is the term used when referring to liquids or other materials which can be poured. Capacity is generally measured in litres (l) and millilitres (ml). It is important to note that 1 cubic centimetre is equal to 1 millilitre. Many of the activities in this chapter relate to capacity as this is the most likely form in which the children will encounter the concept in everyday life. However, many of the activities can easily be adapted to explore volume.

Because of the nature of the activities and the use of materials such as sand and water, some mess must be expected. To alleviate some of the problems that may occur, try:

• working in small groups (three or four children)
• when working with sand, keeping a small dustpan and brush available so the children can clean up any spillage themselves
• when working with water, keeping an absorbent cloth available for cleaning up
• telling the children that you expect very little or no mess and that they are responsible for cleaning up
• demonstrating how to fill a container by leaning over another container which will catch any spillage
• avoiding the use of glass altogether

Full or empty? It is best to introduce this activity with two groups of containers, some as examples of 'full' and others as examples of 'empty'. The children could sort them accordingly.
Half-full Before starting this activity the children must have some idea of what 'half' means. It is important to be aware that younger or less able children may only realise that a container is neither full nor empty, with no concept of the fractions in between. Older or more able children may realise that 'half-full' and 'half-empty' mean the same thing.
Which holds most? This activity involves comparing the capacities of three different containers. The children can use either sand or water for the pouring. They will have to make sure each container is full before pouring its contents into the next one.
Cupfuls This activity uses cups of water (or sand) as a non-standard unit of measurement. You will need a collection of containers and additional cups.
How many? This activity explores the appropriateness of using various non-standard

units. At the end, discuss which small container the children think is the most appropriate.
❏ Suggest a different large container to be measured. Does the choice of small container change? Why?

New paint Be prepared for some successes, some failures and some mess! Emphasise that the children do not have to use all the ingredients.
❏ Make the results into a display.

Litres This activity explores 1l as a standard unit of measurement. Fill each of the smaller containers and then pour the contents into the litre measure to find its capacity.

Make a litre This activity explores the actual quantity of liquid needed to make a litre and further develops the children's estimation skills relating to litres.
❏ Try the same activity using a 500ml container.

More or less? There may be more than one acceptable answer for some of the containers.
❏ The children could add a picture of their own to each box.

Halves and quarters For this activity you will need to supply a set of containers that will each hold less than 1l, a 1l jug and some water (or sand). The second part of the activity looks at adding ¼l, ½l and ¾l. The children may need to do this practically.

Spoons You will need to have a variety of spoons available. If the children bring them from home, make sure they are labelled. Try to include serving spoons and ladles. You will need several of each type for the second part of the activity.

Evaporation This activity would relate well to a Science unit on 'The water cycle'. Try to leave the containers in a sunny place. The children should discover that the water in the narrower containers evaporates more slowly than that in the wider containers.
❏ The water could be made salty to show the effects of evaporation.

Reading a scale 1 This activity allows the children to practise reading a scale. Discuss some ways of working out what each mark on a scale could mean.

Reading a scale 2 Have measuring containers with scales on them available for this estimating activity. If the children bring plastic measuring jugs from home, make sure they are labelled.

Litres and millilitres The children must be able to convert from litres to millilitres and from millilitres to litres: 1000ml = 1l.
Answers: 1l, ½l, 2¼l, 1⅕l, ⅕l, 1½l, ¼l, 500ml, 500ml, 250ml, 2500ml, 100ml, 1000ml, 200ml.

Cooking This activity allows the children to practise converting Imperial units to metric units.
❏ Try making punch with the class. Use the different recipes which the children have invented. Then have a tasting.
Answers: 570ml, 275ml, 275ml, 425ml, 55ml, 150ml.

Pints and gallons This activity explores the relationship between two Imperial measures still in use: the pint and the gallon.

Volume problems (cards) This activity sheet can be cut up into six separate problem cards for individual or group work.
❏ The children could make up some problems of their own for others to solve.

Boxes This activity explores using centicubes to measure volume. You will need to provide boxes of different shapes and sizes and lots of centicubes.

Lids This activity will allow the children to practise measuring small volumes with increasing accuracy. You will need to provide a collection of lids of different shapes and sizes.

In the shops This activity explores the fact that containers which hold the same amount can be different shapes, and the reasons why there are differences.
❏ Make a class collection of containers which hold 1l.

Cubes This activity helps the children to visualise cubes within a solid shape and to explore the volume of solid shapes which are not cubes/cuboids.
❏ The children could make their own shapes with cubes and try to draw them on isometric (triangle dotted) paper.

Cubes and cuboids The children must know how to calculate the volume of a cube/cuboid and express it in cm^3.
Answers: A $126cm^3$, B $4cm^3$, C $45cm^3$, D $135cm^3$, E $27cm^3$, $144cm^3$.

Capacity and volume This activity explores the relationship between volume (cubic centimetres) and capacity (millilitres). The children should discover that $1cm^3 = 1ml$.

Time

Night and day This activity asks the children to sort a set of pictures into two groups, those which show night-time scenes and those which show daytime scenes.

After school This activity asks the children to place events in time sequence.
❏ The children could illustrate and write, if possible, the sequence of their morning routine, a weekend, a school day or a school week.

O'clock This activity requires the children to practise telling the time in whole hours. As an introductory activity, encourage them to practise telling the time in whole hours using real clocks.

Days of the week
❏ Make a class big book called 'A week in the life of Class ___'. Add a new page each day.
Making clocks This activity focuses on the position of each number on the clock face.
The seasons This sheet looks at different activities and scenes that take place during each of the seasons. The children could also write the names of the relevant months in each column.
The calendar 1 and 2 You will need to prepare a set of calendar pages for each month.
❏ Appropriate activities/questions can be set for each month linking to the cultural diversity of the class. For example, on what day did Ramadan start?
Birthdays This activity asks the children to show on a block graph the month of birth of each class member. Some previous experience of graphing is necessary.
Timing devices This activity explores non-standard units of time and shows that 'time' is a human concept.
Telling the time The children will need to have had an explanation of telling the time in 5-minute intervals before attempting this worksheet.
On time This activity uses both digital and analogue clock faces.
Answers: 9.20, 4.25, 1 hour 5 minutes, 6.30.
❏ Use a set of child-made clocks to make a departure board display. The times can be adjusted each day and the children can set or be set questions relating to the display.
TV times This activity looks further at how time is recorded and calculated. For the sorting, you will need to provide TV magazines or newspapers giving the times of programmes on a Monday. You will need to emphasise that the children must decide on the most appropriate categories.

❏ They could go on to do this activity for an entire week.
In a minute This sheet could be used in conjunction with a game of 'Guess a minute'. All the children stand, and after the word 'Go' they sit down when they think a minute has passed. This leads on to thinking of and trying out different ways of calculating a minute.
Matching For this activity, the children must be able to tell the time on both analogue and digital clocks to 5-minute intervals.
Writing the date This activity explores the conventions used for recording dates.
❏ Encourage the children to practise writing the date on their work, using a different style each week.
Morning and afternoon This activity explores the conventions of recording time using 'a.m.' or 'p.m.'
Seconds This activity uses a stopwatch to time various tasks in seconds. You may need to demonstrate the use of a stopwatch if the children have not used one before. Remind the children that the watch must be reset for each activity.
24-hour clocks An explanation will be needed if this is the children's first encounter with 24-hour time. It may be useful to make a timeline for one day using 24-hour time.
Tickets The children will need to be familiar with 24-hour time.
❏ Make a collection of real tickets and ask the children to explain the times on them. Each child could make up his or her own ticket and then ask a friend to explain the times on it.
Triathlon times The children will need to have had some experience of calculating duration in minutes. They could go on to convert the answers into hours and minutes or digital times.

Babysitting You may need to revise the concept of rounding up. Extra paper may be needed for the working out in this activity.
Answers:

Hunter	3.30	3.30	£8.50
Stephens	5.15	5.15	£13.00
MacLeod	2.52	3	£7.50
Jones	4	4	£10.00
Hunter	6.21	6.30	£16.00
Hunter	11.18	11.30	£28.50
MacLeod	1.14	1.15	£3.00
Jones	6.02	6.15	£15.50
Jones	6.40	6.45	£16.50
Hunter	6.06	6.15	£15.50

Total earnings £134.00
Hunter £68.50
Stephens £13.00
MacLeod £10.50
Jones £42.00
Best client: Hunter

Speed This activity sets up a practical situation for calculating and recording speed. You may need to give an example to show how to calculate speed, and explain the units used.

Perimeter

How far round? This activity asks children to identify the perimeter of an image, and to compare the perimeters of pairs of images by eye. Make sure they understand the term 'distance around'.
Answers: football pitch, envelope, classroom, hopscotch.
Measuring perimeters This activity involves estimating and measuring perimeters as well as choosing the most appropriate measuring device and units.
Solve the riddle The children will need to know how to find the perimeter of a shape by adding lengths.

Answer: Without it, it would be a sick insect.

Borders

❑ In small groups, the children could design and make new borders for each display board in the classroom. They could relate them to their current topic, and use a variety of media.

Squares This activity asks the children to find the perimeters of different squares by adding side lengths. It goes on to explore easier ways of finding the perimeter of a square. The children should realise that you can multiply the side length by 4. It may be useful to talk about the properties of a square beforehand.

Answers: 4cm, 8cm, 12cm, 16cm, 20cm.

Rectangles This activity asks the children to find the perimeters of different rectangles by adding side lengths. It goes on to explore easier ways of finding the perimeter of a rectangle. The children may realise that you can add one long side length to one short side length and multiply by 2. It may be useful to review the properties of a rectangle, especially the lengths of the sides, beforehand.

Answers: 10cm, 18cm, 22cm, 24cm.

Christmas lights

❑ The children could make their own Christmas shape using cardboard and decorate it with tinsel. They will have to calculate how much tinsel they will require.

Swimming pools This activity requires the children to calculate perimeters by adding lengths.

Answers: A 38m £855, B 70m £1575, C 92m £2070.

❑ How much would it cost to replace the fencing around the school playing fields?

Squared paper This activity asks the children to draw different shapes each with a perimeter of 16cm.

❑ The children could go on to find the area of each shape and make comparisons.

Regular polygons This activity explores the use of addition or multiplication to find the perimeters of different regular polygons. Before starting, it may be useful to discuss the properties of a regular polygon.

Answers: triangle 12cm, square 20cm, pentagon 15cm, hexagon 12cm, heptagon 7cm, octagon 12cm.

Different shapes

❑ The children could also find as many rectangles as they can with a perimeter of 24cm. This could be related to work on factors. The measurement can be altered for variety.

On the farm Make the children aware of the fact that not all the measurements needed for this activity are given and that some will need to be calculated. You may need to explain about 'grants'. Be aware that this activity also includes a percentage calculation.

Answers: Total fencing: 6000m; total cost: £111,000; Farmer Donald's bill: £49,950.

Doubling up This activity investigates the effect on perimeter of doubling and then tripling the side lengths of a rectangle. Discuss 'doubling' and 'tripling'. Encourage the children to use different coloured pencils for the rectangles in case they overlap.

Answers: A 10cm, B 20cm, C 30cm, D 40cm.

Lakes Measuring irregular perimeters requires careful use of the measuring device. For smaller perimeters string is useful, and for larger shapes a trundle wheel is probably the most suitable device to use.

Answer: Lake Hawthorn.

❑ Measure the perimeter of a puddle at different times during the day. Discuss the results.

Perimeter problems (cards) This page provides six problem cards to be given to individuals or pairs of children and then swapped.

❑ Encourage the children to go on to make up perimeter problems for each other to solve.

Find the perimeter The children will need to know how to convert between metres, centimetres and kilometres before attempting this sheet. Watch out for children who try to add up the measurements without first converting them to common units.

Answers: A 3486m, B 2900m, C 20000m, D 157.9km, E 642m, F 3334m.

Joining shapes This activity explores placing two shapes together to make a new shape and then calculating the new perimeter. Different ways of connecting the shapes will produce different perimeters.

Answers: A 16cm, B 12cm, C 14cm, D 16cm; A and D have the same perimeter.

❑ Ask the children to find the combination which produces the smallest/largest perimeter.

Athletics This activity develops work on the perimeter of a rectangle.

Answers: less than one, less than one, less than one, one and a bit, two and a bit, three and a bit, thirteen and a bit, twenty-seven and a bit.

❑ Do the exercise again based on the measurements of your school field. Discuss why there are staggered starts at real athletics events.

Warm-up As an introduction or follow-up, work out how far the children would run if they jogged around the school playing field. How many laps would they have to do to run 1km?

Answers: 208.44m, 274.5m, 219.6m, 144m. The netball player runs furthest. The volleyball player runs the least distance. 347.4m, 457.5m, 366m, 240m. No one runs further than 1km.

Circles The children should realise that the diameter will fit 'three and a bit' times around the circumference of a circle. If you divide the circumference (**c**) of any circle by its diameter (**d**), the result is ≈ 3.14. This number is known as pi and its symbol is π. Therefore **c = πd**.
Answers:
A 2cm 4cm 12.56cm
B 3cm 6cm 18.84cm
C 4cm 8cm 25.12cm
D 5cm 10cm 31.4cm

Area

Large and small This activity assumes understanding of the term 'area'.
Answers: playing field, blanket, book, £5 note.
Larger or smaller? The children could write their lists or give them orally.
❏ Make other lists, for example, objects which have an area greater than that of a £5 note.
Measuring with blocks This activity and the two following ones start to explore non-standard units of different sizes and their suitability for measuring increasingly large areas.
Measuring with books The children may need to use such terms as 'a bit more than', 'about' and 'a bit less than' to describe the areas covered by the books.
Measuring with newspaper The children need to have measured area using smaller non-standard units before attempting this activity. When measuring larger areas the children could work in a small group and use just one sheet of newspaper and a piece of chalk. They trace round the sheet of newspaper and count the resulting number of squares/rectangles.
Geoboards This activity asks children to make three different shapes with an area of six square units. You can use any size of geoboard.
❏ The children could find the shape on the geoboard with the greatest/smallest area.
Alphabet area This activity asks children to find the areas of various letters of the alphabet in square centimetres.
Answers: L 10cm², E 15cm², T 11cm².
Hands The class will need to share their results in order to complete the table.
Leaves The children may need extra squared paper if they are using large leaves. This activity can be adapted to suit any group of flat objects.
Square centimetres You may have to provide more squared paper depending on the size of the objects chosen. The children will need to have had some experience of counting parts of squares before attempting this activity.
Find the area This sheet could be used for assessment.
Answers: 7cm², 5cm², 22cm², 8cm². The placemat has an area of 38cm².
Square metres The children will have to work co-operatively to measure the larger areas. They could use chalk to trace around the square metre and then count the squares.
Designing a garden This activity explores different ways of making an area of 12 square metres. Encourage a variety of ideas including separate areas that add up to 12 square metres.
Blackout! This activity could be linked to the History unit of study 'Britain since 1930'.
❏ The children could work out how much material would be required to black out their homes, and how much it would cost.
Squares This activity investigates finding the area of a square using length × breadth. Explain what is meant by 'number of rows' and 'number of squares in each row'.
Answers: 4, 4, 16; 6, 6, 36; 8, 8, 64; 12, 12, 144; 196cm².
Rectangles Compare the results of this worksheet with those of 'Squares' on page 137. Discuss any similarities or differences.
Answers: 4, 10, 40; 12, 6, 72; 6, 22, 132; 72cm².
Gardens Demonstrate how to divide each shape into squares, rectangles or a combination of both.
Answers: Mr Akram 16m², Mr Bourke 46m², Mr Skipton 12.5m², Mrs Kimptos 26m²; total area 100.5m².
Right-angled triangles You may have to show more examples of right-angled triangles and the associated squares/rectangles before the children realise that the area of the triangle is half the area of the square/rectangle.
Answers: A 16cm² 8cm², B 9cm² 4.5cm², C 12cm² 6cm², D 36cm² 18cm², E 24cm² 12cm².
One into two This activity develops the activity 'Right-angled triangles' on page 140. As in the 'Gardens' activity on page 139 the children are investigating combinations of areas to find a total.
Answers: A 7.5cm², B 16cm², C 8cm², D 20cm², E 17.5cm².
Kites The children will need to know how to find the area of a right-angled triangle to complete this sheet.
Answer: B.
New carpets The cost per metre for carpet/linoleum is left blank on this sheet so that you can choose amounts appropriate to the children's ability (with or without decimal points).
❏ The children could go on to find out the cost of new carpet for their school.
Measuring farmland Discuss when it may be appropriate to use square kilometres as a unit of measurement.

Links with the UK curricula for Mathematics

England and Wales: Mathematics in the National Curriculum

The activities in this book support the following requirements of the Programmes of Study:

Key Stage 1: Shape, space and measures
- Pupils should be given opportunities to:
* gain a wide range of practical experience using a variety of materials
* use purposeful contexts for measuring
- Pupils should be taught to:

a compare objects and events using appropriate language, by direct comparison, and then using common non-standard and standard units of length, mass and capacity, e.g. 'three-and-a-bit metres long', 'as heavy as 10 conkers', about three beakers full'; begin to use a wider range of standard units, including standard units of time, choosing units appropriate to a situation; estimate with these units

b choose and use simple measuring instruments, reading and interpreting numbers and scales with some accuracy

Key Stage 2: Shape, space and measures
- Pupils should be given opportunities to:
* extend their practical experience using a wide range of materials
* apply their measuring skills in a range of purposeful contexts
- Pupils should be taught to:

a choose appropriate standard units of length, mass, capacity and time, and make sensible estimates with them in everyday situations; extend their understanding of the relationship between units; convert one metric unit to another; know the rough metric equivalents of Imperial units still in daily use

b choose and use appropriate measuring instruments; interpret numbers and read scales to an increasing degree of accuracy

c find perimeters of simple shapes; find practically the circumferences of circles, being introduced to the ratio π; find areas and volumes by counting methods

Northern Ireland: Mathematics Programmes of Study and Attainment Targets

The activities in this book support the following requirements of the Programmes of Study:

Key Stage 1: Measures
- Pupils should have opportunities to:

a compare and order objects, developing and using mathematical language associated with length, 'weight', capacity, area and time

b use non-standard units in length, 'weight', capacity, area and time to measure a range of everyday objects and events, and recognise the need to use standard units

c know the most commonly used units in length, 'weight', capacity and time, including metres, kilograms, litres, hours and minutes, and what they are used for; begin to use a wider range of standard units, for example, cm, ½ kilogram and ½ litre, choosing appropriately for a situation

d sequence everyday events, for example, *breakfast time, lunch time, and teatime*; know that time within a day comprises morning, afternoon, evening, night; know the days of the week, months of the year

e recognise times on the clock face, initially significant times, for example, *lunch time, home time* and progressing to the hour, half-hour and quarter hours; begin to read the five-minute intervals on an analogue clock, compare analogue and digital displays for the hour and half-hour

f make estimates using arbitrary and standard units

g choose and use simple measuring instruments, reading and interpreting them with some accuracy

h understand the conservation of measures

Key Stage 2: Measures
- Pupils should have opportunities to:

a develop skills in estimation of length, 'weight', volume/capacity, time, area and temperature through practical activities, using metric units where appropriate

b develop the language associated with a wider range of metric units and be confident with the terms metre, gram and litre, and the relevant prefixes kilo, cent, milli

c choose and use appropriate metric units and measuring instruments in a variety of situations, interpreting numbers on a range of measuring instruments

d understand the relationship between units, for example, *know that kilograms and grams are used to weigh food*; convert from one metric unit to another, for example *know that 175 centimetres is 1.75 metres*

e know the Imperial units still in common use including foot, yard, mile, pound and pint

g understand the concept of perimeter and calculate the perimeter of simple shapes; find areas by counting squares and volumes by counting cubes, using whole numbers; calculate areas and volumes of simple shapes in two and three dimensions

h understand and use scale in the context of simple maps and drawings, for example, *draw a simple plan of the classroom and know that one centimetre square represents one square metre; calculate the actual distance as the crow flies between two places on a map using the scale of 1cm to 1km*

i know the units of measurement in time and the relationship between them

j recognise times on the analogue clock, including the hour, half and quarter hours, five minute intervals and one minute intervals; understand the relationship between the twelve and twenty-four hour clocks, including a.m. and p.m.; read analogue and digital displays and understand the relationship between them; use timetables involving the twenty-four hour clock and perform simple calculations related to the timetables

k know the months of the year; explore calendar patterns

Scotland: Mathematics 5–14 Guidelines

The activities in this book support the following Attainment Targets:

Attainment Outcome	Strand	Attainment Target	Level
Number, Money and Measurement	Measure and estimate	All Attainment Targets (except Temperature)	A to D
		Estimate measurements: – small lengths in mm – larger lengths in m Read scales on measuring devices including estimating between graduations	E
	Time	All Attainment Targets	A to D
	Perimeter, Formulae, Scales	Calculate the perimeter of simple straight-sided shapes by adding lengths	D
		Calculate using rules: – areas of rectangles and squares – volumes of cubes and cuboids	E

Name _____

Length
Caterpillars

Caterpillars

You will need: scissors, paste.

These two caterpillars are the same length.

♣ Cut out the four caterpillars at the bottom of the page.

♣ Paste each one below the caterpillar that is the same length.

Paste

Paste

Paste

Paste

Cut

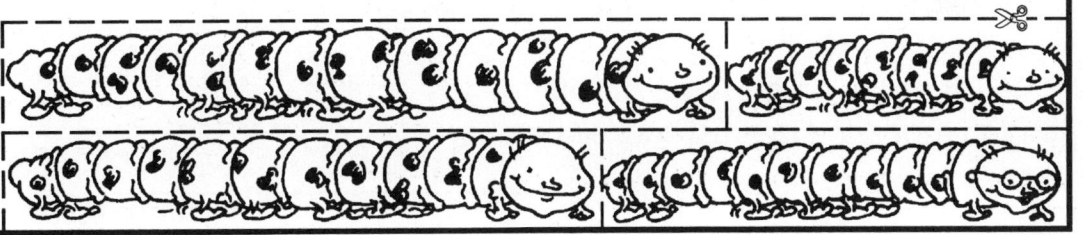

Teacher Timesavers: Measurement skills

Length
As long as

Name _____

As long as

You will need: interlocking cubes such as Unifix or Multilink, Plasticine, a pencil.

♣ Join cubes to make a snake as long as each of these:

♣ Use Plasticine to make a snake as long as your thumb.

♣ Use Plasticine to make the longest snake you can.

♣ Compare it with some of your friends' snakes.
Who made the longest snake?

_____

Name _____

Length
Me

Me

♣ Draw a picture in each box.

Shorter than me	This is me	Taller than me

Teacher Timesavers: Measurement skills

Length
Aliens

Name _____

Aliens

You will need: coloured pencils, scissors, paste, paper.

♣ Look carefully at these aliens.
♣ Colour the shortest alien blue.
Colour the tallest alien red.

Cut ✂

Draw another alien here.

♣ Cut out all the aliens.

♣ Put them in order of height, from shortest to tallest. Paste them on to a sheet of paper in this order.

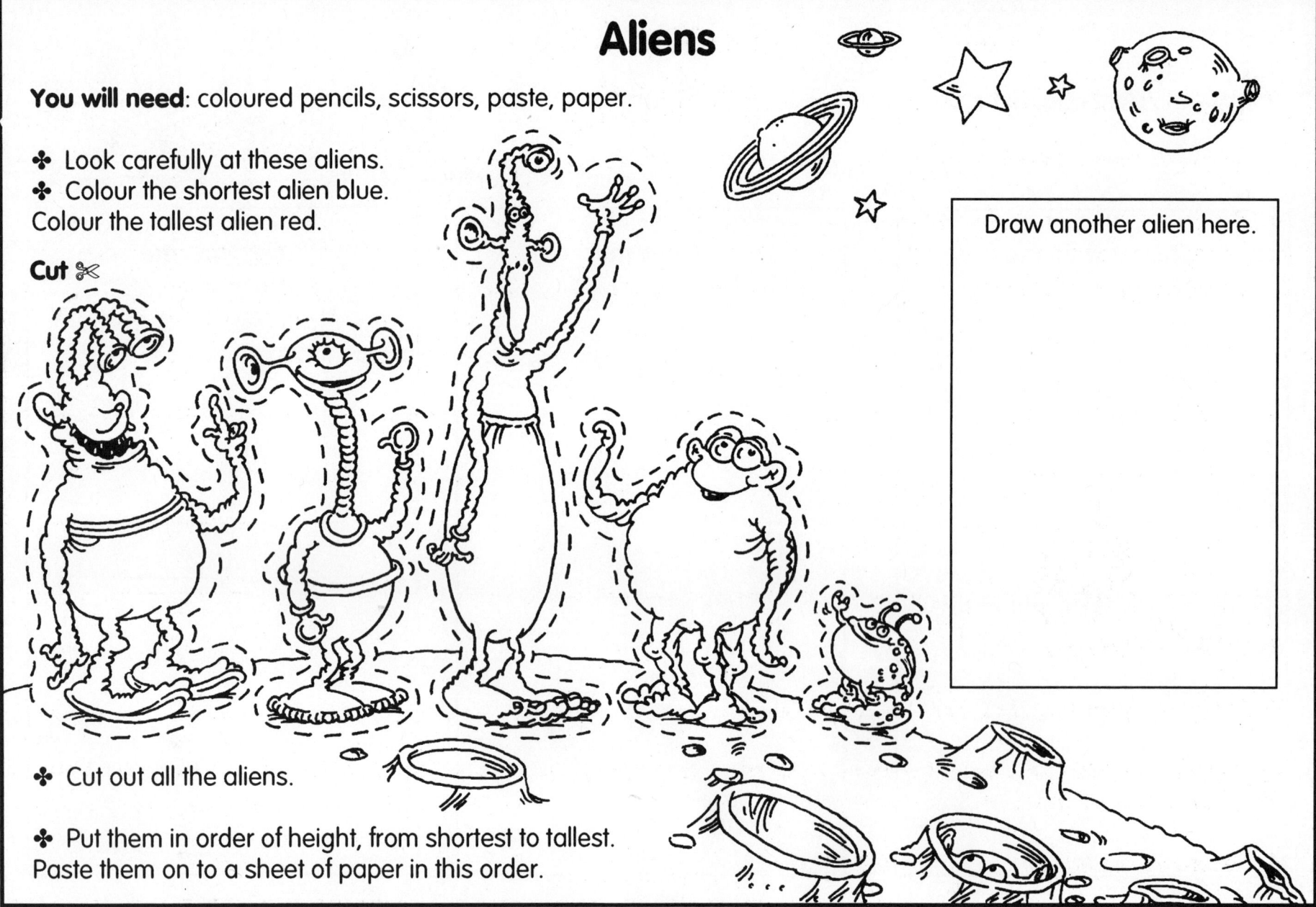

16   Teacher Timesavers: Measurement skills

Name _____

Length

Paperclips

Paperclips

You will need: paperclips, a pencil.

✤ Link together ten paperclips to make a measuring chain.

✤ Use your measuring chain to find:

Five items longer than it	Five items shorter than it	Five items about the same length as it
_____	_____	_____
_____	_____	_____
_____	_____	_____
_____	_____	_____
_____	_____	_____

✤ List the items in the boxes.

✤ Join your measuring chain to that of a friend.

✤ Use your new long measuring chain to find three items longer than it, three items shorter than it and three items about the same length as it.

✤ Record your work on the back of this sheet.

Teacher Timesavers: Measurement skills

Length

What shall I use?

Name _____

What shall I use?

You will need: building blocks, straws, a piece of string, a pencil.

These things can all be used for measuring length:

      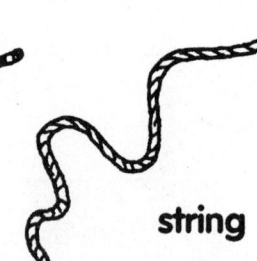   

blocks   **straws**   **string**   **strides**

♣ Measure the items listed in the table.
Choose the most appropriate measuring device from those shown above.

♣ Write your answers in the table.

Item to be measured	Measuring device used	Answer	Did you choose the most appropriate measuring device? Explain.
length of a desk/table			
width of a book			
my wrist			
distance to lunch room			
length of a pencil			
height of a chair			

Teacher Timesavers: Measurement skills

Name _____

Length

Measuring with hands and feet

Measuring with hands and feet

These pictures show some of the different ways in which we can use parts of our bodies for measuring.

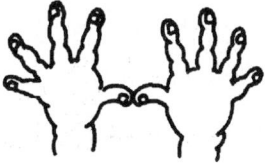   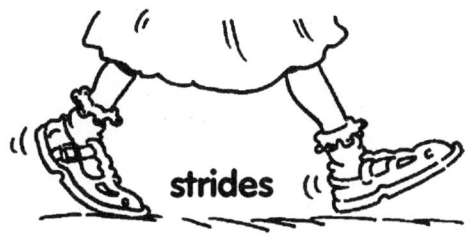   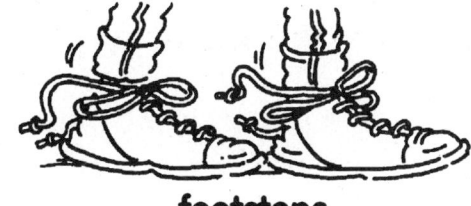   

handspans   **strides**   **footsteps**   **fingerspaces**

❖ Measure the items listed in the table, using the most appropriate body part.

❖ Write your answers in the table.

❖ Choose five other items to measure.

❖ Write your answers in the table.

❖ Compare your answers with those of your friends.

Were your answers the same? _____
Why?/Why not?

_____

_____

_____

Item to be measured	Body part used	Answer
length of a pencil		
height of a desk/table		
distance from my desk/table to the teacher's desk		
width of a door		
distance from classroom to school office		

Teacher Timesavers: Measurement skills

Length
A metre

A metre

You will need: a 1m string, a ½m string, a pencil.

✤ Use a 1m string to measure the items listed in the table.

✤ Complete the table by placing a tick (✓) in the most appropriate column.

Item to be measured	More than 1m	Less than 1m	About 1m
my height			
around a PE hoop			
length of a chalkboard			
width of a window			
height of a doorway			
width of a door			
height of school fence			

✤ Make another list of items to be measured on the back of this sheet.

✤ Use a ½m string to measure them.

✤ State whether each item measures more than ½m, less than ½m or about ½m.

Teacher Timesavers: Measurement skills

Name _____

Length
Snails

Snails

You will need: a centimetre ruler, a pencil.

In this snail race, the snail that covered the greatest distance was the winner.

♣ Use a ruler to measure the distance covered by each snail.

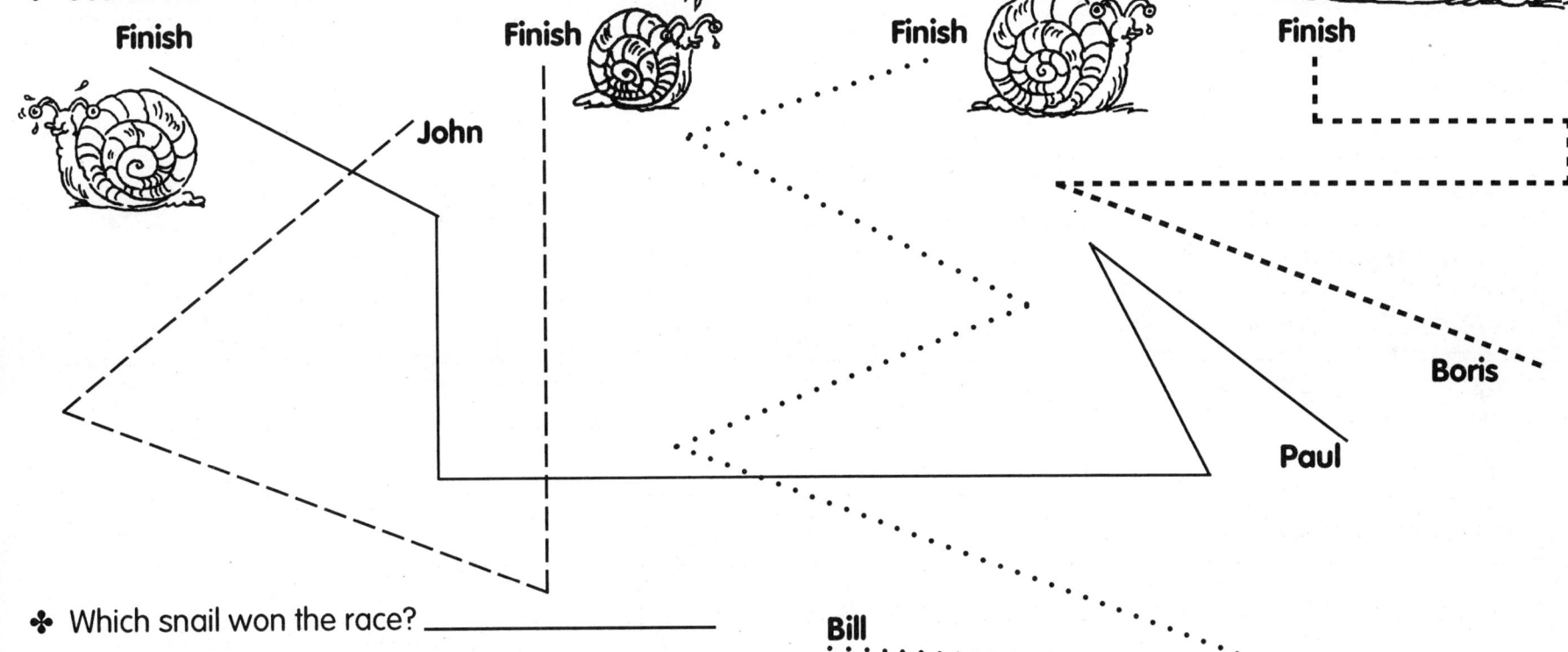

♣ Which snail won the race? _____

♣ Put the snails in order from first to fourth.

1st _____ 2nd _____ 3rd _____ 4th _____

Length
Round and round

Name _____

Round and round

You will need: a piece of string, a centimetre ruler, a pencil.

✤ Use a piece of string and a ruler to measure round six cylindrical objects.

✤ In each box, draw one of the objects and record your measurement.

 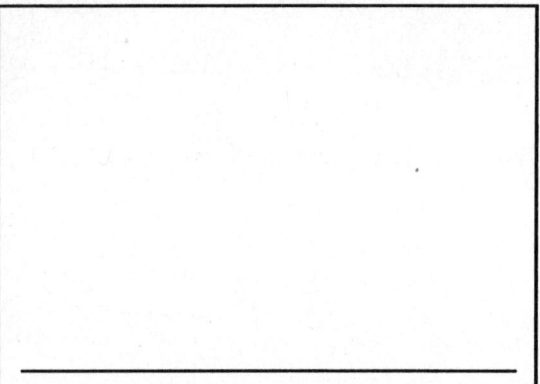

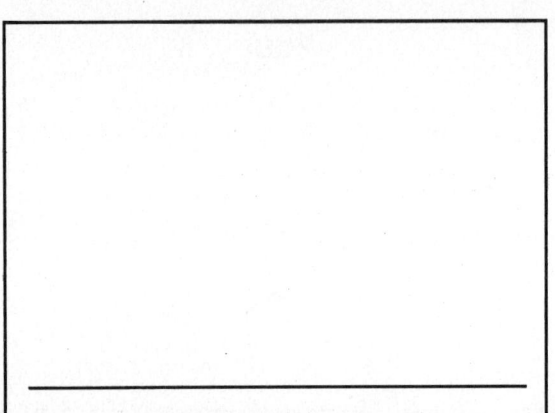 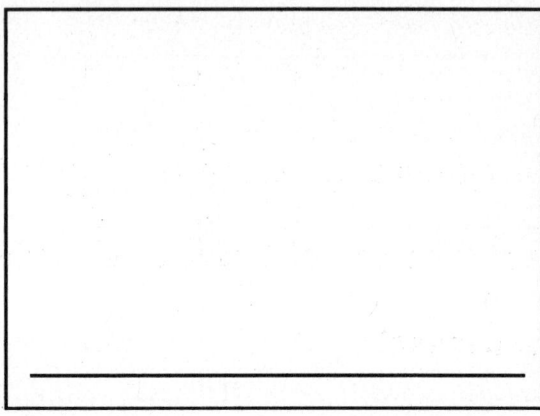 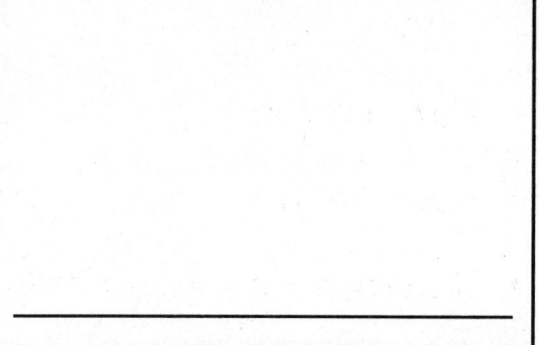

Name _____

Length
Make a metre

Make a metre

A game for two players

You will need: a metre ruler, a centimetre ruler, scissors, card, coloured pencils, a Multilink or Unifix cube, sticky tape.

- Work with a partner.

- Use the metre ruler to make a 1m strip from card.

- Use these labels and some sticky tape to turn your cube into a dice.

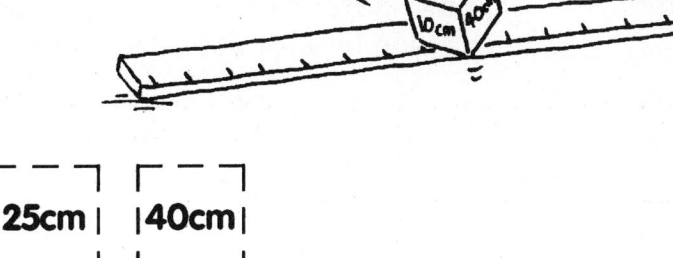

Cut

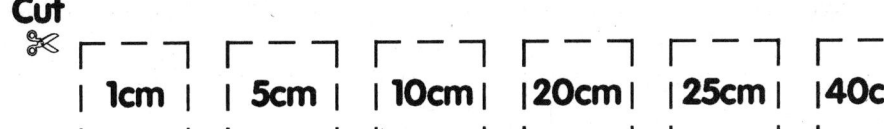

| 1cm | | 5cm | | 10cm | | 20cm | | 25cm | | 40cm |

- Player 1 throws the dice and marks the distance shown (using a centimetre ruler) on the metre strip.

- Player 2 then has a turn, marking the distance in a different colour, and so on.

- The winner is the first person to 'make a metre'.

Teacher Timesavers: Measurement skills

Length

The estimating game

Name _____

The estimating game

A game for two or more players

You will need: paper, pencils, a range of measuring devices, scissors.

- Cut out the cards.
- Place the cards face down on the table.
- A card is chosen and each player records his or her estimate of the answer.
- The object is then measured and a point is awarded to the player with the closest estimate.
- The winner is the player with the most points when all the cards have been used.

Cut ✂

How high is a desk?	Who is the tallest person in your class?	Draw a line 8cm long without using a ruler.	How long is the chalkboard?
What is the perimeter of the playing field?	How wide is the doorway?	Cut a piece of string 1¼m long.	What is the length of a pencil?
How long is a shoelace?	What is the height of your teacher's desk?	How far can one of you jump?	Cut a piece of paper into a rectangular shape 18 cm × 6cm.
How many metres is it to the school office?	How long is a tie?	How high is the ceiling?	How long is your teacher's signature?

Teacher Timesavers: Measurement skills

Name _____   Length

Jumps

Jumps

You will need: a metre ruler, a pencil.

✤ Work in a group of six.

✤ Measure the height of each person and how far he or she can jump. Make sure everyone begins the jump with both feet together.

✤ Record your results in the table.

✤ Now answer these questions.

• Who is the tallest person? _____

• Who is the shortest person? _____

• Does the tallest person have the longest jump?

_____

• Does the shortest person have the shortest jump?

_____

Name	Height	Length of jump

Teacher Timesavers: Measurement skills

Length

A long journey

Name _____

A long journey

A game for two players

You will need: scissors, pencils, paper.

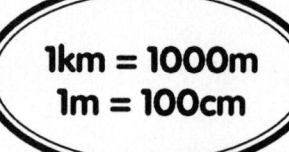

1km = 1000m
1m = 100cm

- Cut out the cards and place them face down.

- Pretend that you are two runners in a 5km race.
The winner is the first person to reach 5km, using the cards.

- Take it in turns to choose a card and record the distance it shows.
You will need to convert centimetres to metres, and metres to kilometres, as you build up your distance.

Cut

10cm	1550m	2260m	4km 20m	10m	2½km	600m	90cm
1km	20cm	2500m	250m	500m	4500m	80cm	100cm
1500m	2km	30cm	1¾m	1½km	700m	1m	½km
3km 40m	1½m	3km	40cm	3500m	900m	70cm	3½km
500m	504m	3km 80m	4km	½m	200m	40m	300m
1¼m	2km 50m	1km 70m	750m	100m	60cm	4½km	400m

Teacher Timesavers: Measurement skills

Name _____

Length

How far?

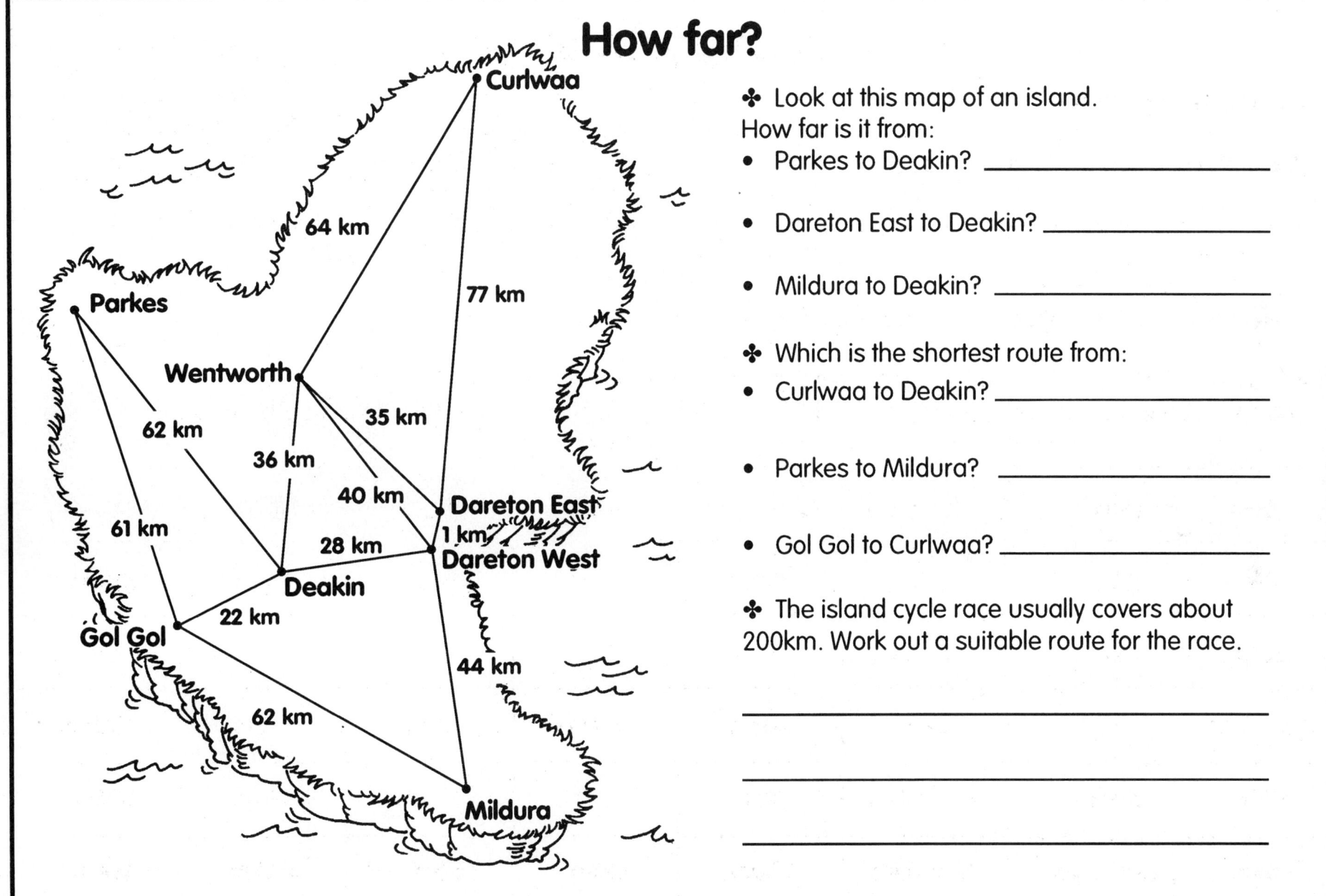

How far?

✤ Look at this map of an island.
How far is it from:
- Parkes to Deakin? _____

- Dareton East to Deakin? _____

- Mildura to Deakin? _____

✤ Which is the shortest route from:
- Curlwaa to Deakin? _____

- Parkes to Mildura? _____

- Gol Gol to Curlwaa? _____

✤ The island cycle race usually covers about 200km. Work out a suitable route for the race.

_____

_____

_____

Teacher Timesavers: Measurement skills

Sports

You will need: a trundle wheel, a pencil.

Imagine that your school is going to have some new courts for playing various sports. This table shows the measurements of the courts.

Sport	Length of court (m)	Width of court (m)
tennis	23.77	10.97
football	90	45
volleyball	18	9
netball	30.5	15.25
badminton	13.4	6.1

♣ Measure your school's playing area.
♣ Draw it on the back of this sheet, marking all the measurements you have made.

♣ Which courts will fit into the playing area? _____

To accommodate spectators, another 2m will have to be added to the length and width of all courts.

♣ Which courts will fit into the playing area now? _____
Draw them on your plan.

♣ Conduct a survey to find out which courts would be the most popular. List them from most popular to least popular.

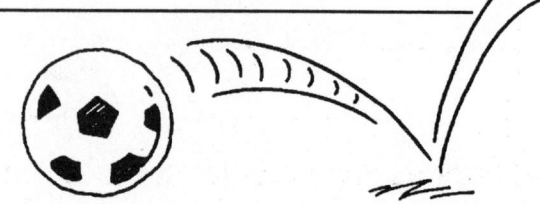

Name _____

Length
Millimetres

Millimetres

You will need: a millimetre ruler, a pencil.

✤ Measure the items listed in the table using millimetres (mm).

✤ Write down your estimates first.

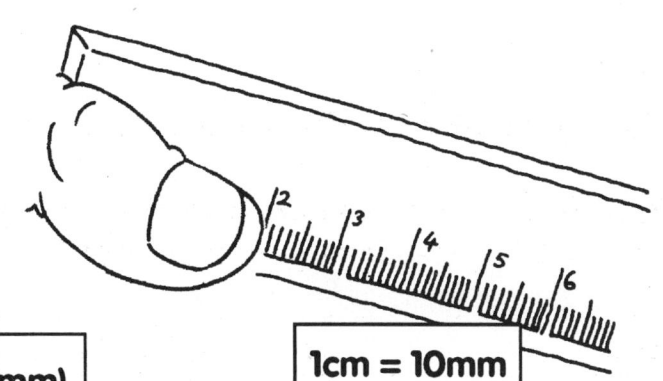

1cm = 10mm

Item to be measured	Estimate (mm)	Measurement (mm)
width of an eraser		
width of a piece of string		
width of a pencil		
diameter of a punched hole		
length of my thumbnail		

✤ Complete this table:

cm	mm
30	
25	
12	
4	
½	
36	
18	
5	
135	
450	

✤ Choose some other items to measure to complete the table.

Teacher Timesavers: Measurement skills

Length
Dinosaur fun

Name _____

Dinosaur fun

You will need: a centimetre ruler, a pencil.

The diagram below shows the positions of some dinosaurs which have been discovered by scientists.

Help the scientists to find out how far apart the dinosaurs are.

♣ Use a centimetre ruler to measure the distance between the dinosaurs in each pair listed below. Use the scale to convert the distances to kilometres.

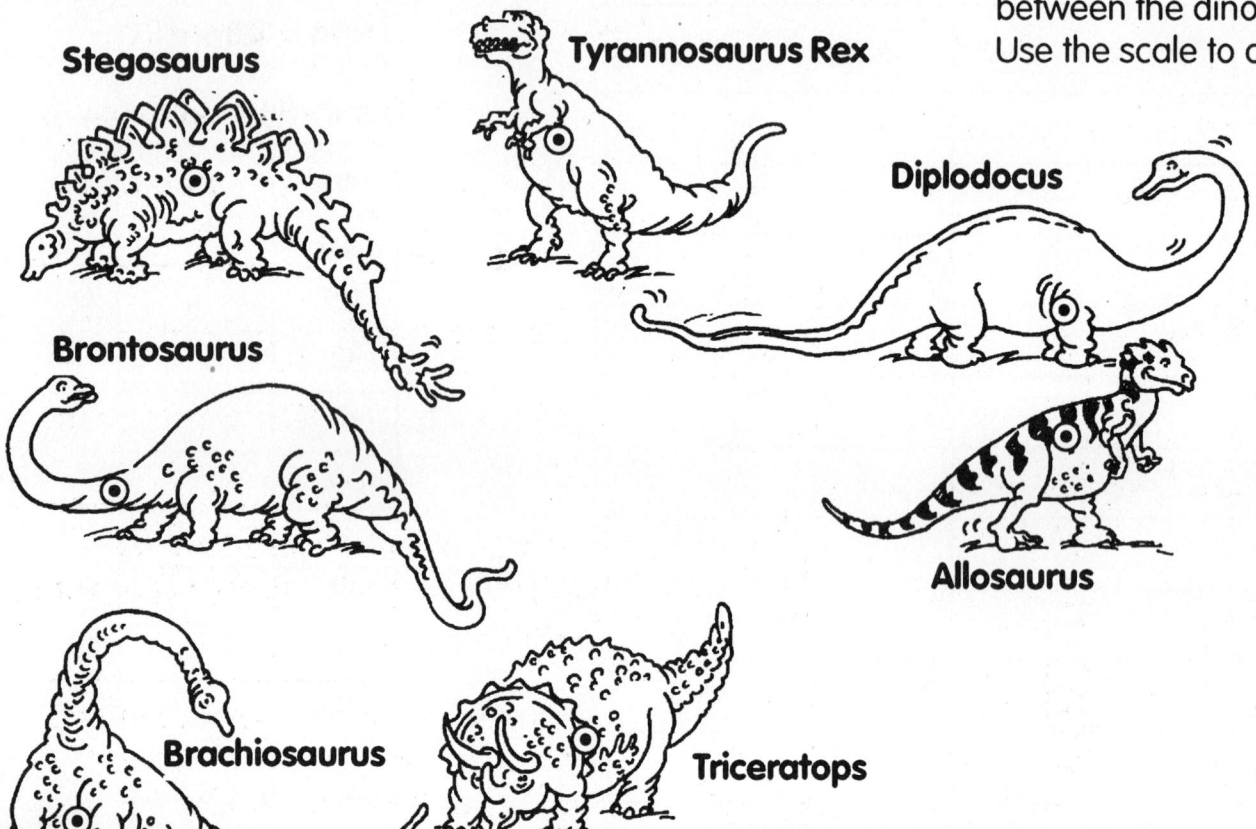

- Stegosaurus/Diplodocus
  _____

- Tyrannosaurus Rex/Triceratops
  _____

- Brontosaurus/Allosaurus
  _____

- Tyrannosaurus Rex/Allosaurus
  _____

- Brachiosaurus/Triceratops
  _____

Scale: 1cm = 1km

Teacher Timesavers: Measurement skills

Name _____

Length
Scale

Scale

You will need: a centimetre ruler, a pencil.

This railway map has a scale of 1cm = 8km.
This means that 1cm on the map equals 8km in real life.

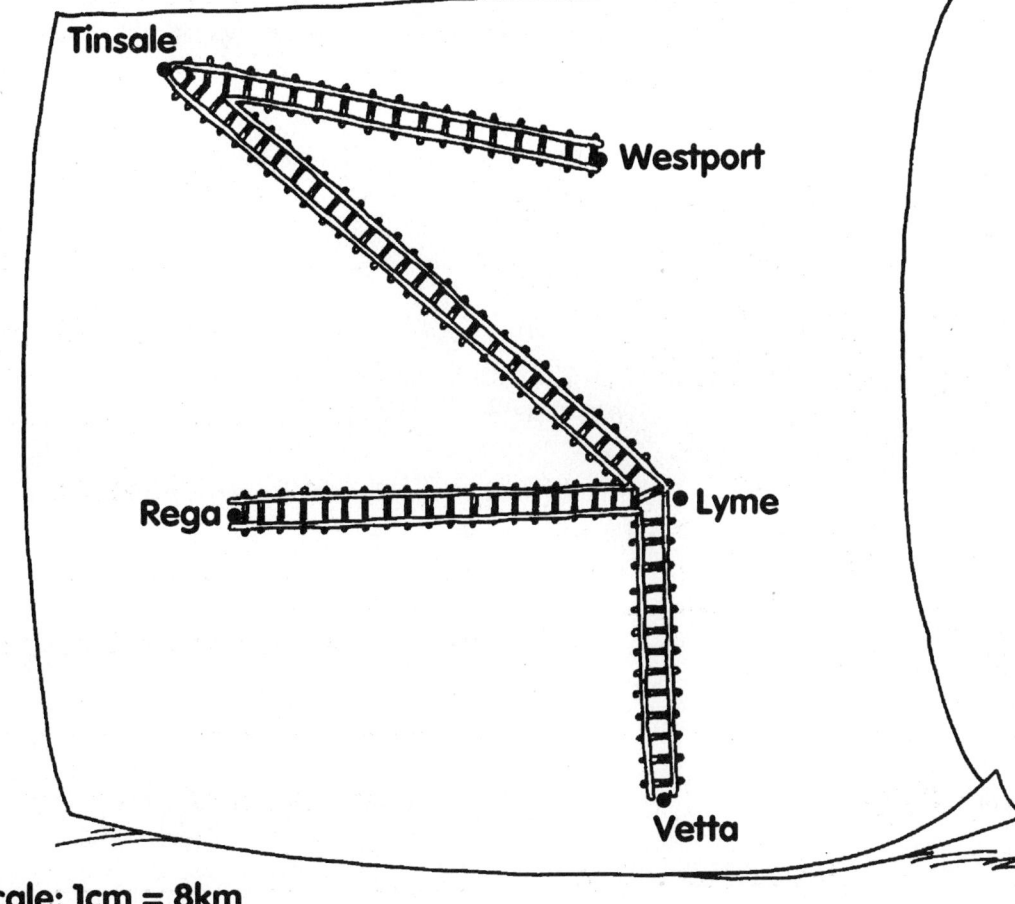

Scale: 1cm = 8km

♣ Answer these questions about the map.
Measure each distance to the nearest centimetre.

- How far is it in kilometres from:

    Tinsale to Westport? _____

    Westport to Lyme? _____

    Tinsale to Rega? _____

    Rega to Vetta? _____

- How far is the return journey from Lyme to Tinsale?
    _____

- If the train travels at 24km per hour, how long will it take to complete this journey?
    _____

- If I start and finish at Westport and plan to visit all the stations marked, how far will I have to travel?
    _____

Teacher Timesavers: Measurement skills

Length
Scale drawing

Name _____

Scale drawing

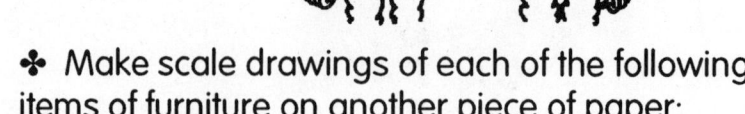

You will need: a centimetre ruler, paper, scissors, paste, a pencil.

This is a plan of the twins' bedroom, drawn to a scale of 1cm = 0.5m.

♣ Make scale drawings of each of the following items of furniture on another piece of paper:

- 2 beds 1.5m × 1m

- 2 desks 1m × 0.5m

- 1 wardrobe 3m × 0.5m

♣ Cut out your drawings and paste them on to the plan of the room in suitable positions.

♣ Make a scale drawing of your own bedroom. Make sure you measure the room and the furniture before you start.

32 Teacher Timesavers: Measurement skills

Name _____

Length

Miles to kilometres

Miles to kilometres

1 mile = 1.609km

A quick and easy way of converting miles into kilometres (approximately) is to multiply by 1½.

For example: 44 miles = 44 + (½ of 44)
= 44 + 22
= 66 km

44 miles is about 66km.

♣ Convert each of these distances to kilometres.

♣ Write the names of the towns in the right spaces.

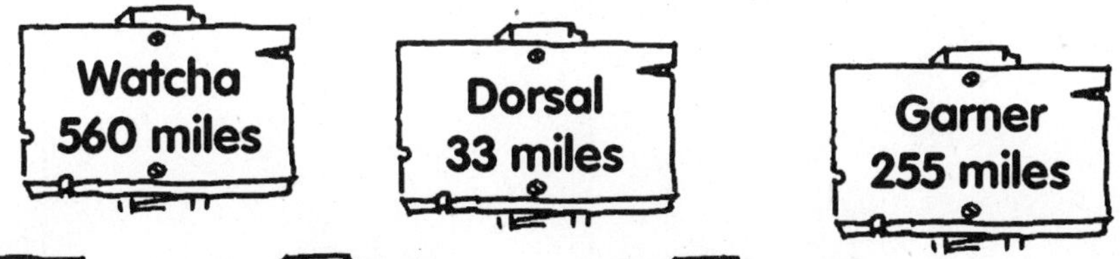

Watcha 560 miles
Dorsal 33 miles
Garner 255 miles
Blimpy 12 miles 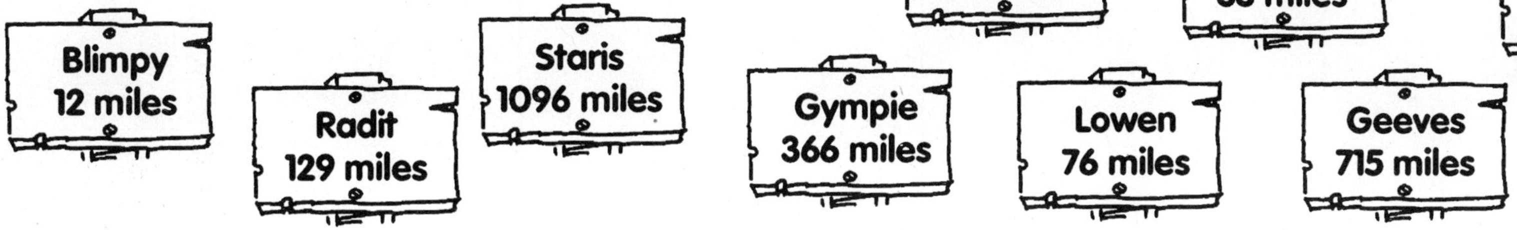
Staris 1096 miles
Radit 129 miles
Gympie 366 miles
Lowen 76 miles
Geeves 715 miles

| _____ | _____ | _____ | _____ | _____ |
| 6km | 1736km | 20km | 1152km | 53km |

| _____ | _____ | _____ | _____ | _____ |
| 902km | 122km | 589km | 208km | 411km |

Teacher Timesavers: Measurement skills

Mass

Name _____

Heavier or lighter?

Heavier or lighter?

You will need: a pencil, scissors, paste.

✤ Cut out the pictures.

✤ Paste each picture in the correct box.

Heavier than me	About the same weight as me	Lighter than me

✤ Draw another object in each box.

Cut ✂

elephant

man

car

pillow

feather

pencil

motor bike

child

baby

clothes peg

dog

Teacher Timesavers: Measurement skills

Name _____

Mass

Using a balance

Using a balance

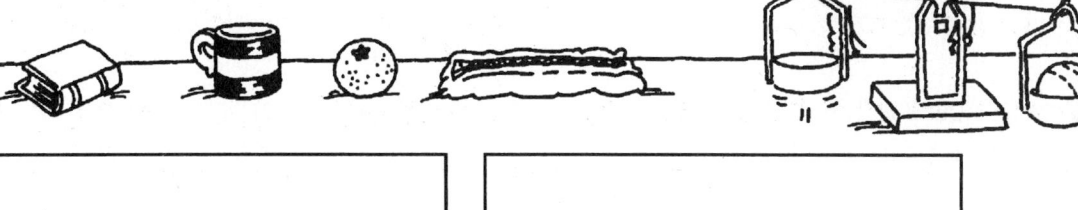

You will need: a collection of small objects, a balance, a pencil.

✣ Choose three objects.

✣ Draw them in the boxes.

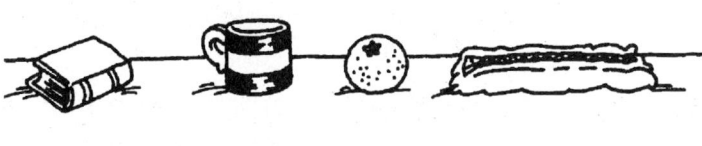

✣ Pick up each object in turn and then answer these questions:

   • Which do you think is the heaviest? _____

   • Which do you think is the lightest? _____

✣ Use a balance to weigh each object in turn.

✣ Draw them again, putting them in order from lightest to heaviest.

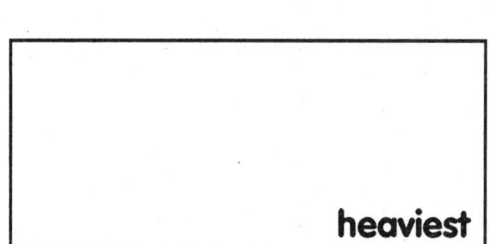

lightest		**heaviest**

✣ Were your guesses correct? _____

Teacher Timesavers: Measurement skills   35

Mass

Which is heavier?

Name _____

Which is heavier?

You will need: a balance, a pencil, the objects shown below.

♣ Pick up each pair of objects in turn.

♣ Which do you think is heavier? Write your answer in the box.

♣ Use a balance to check your predictions.

♣ Draw a circle round the picture of the object that is heavier.

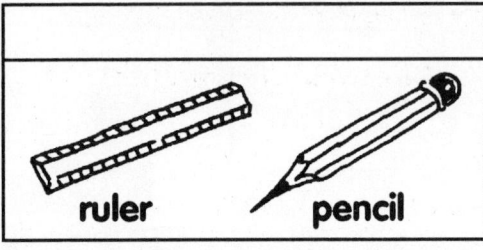

ruler   pencil

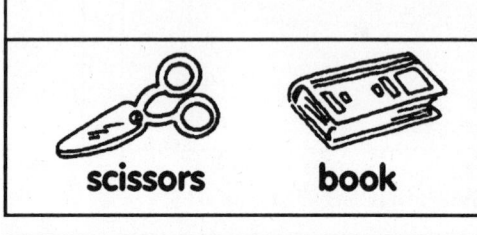

scissors   book

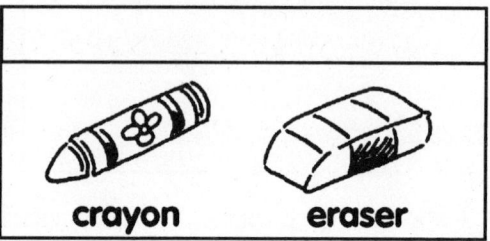

crayon   eraser

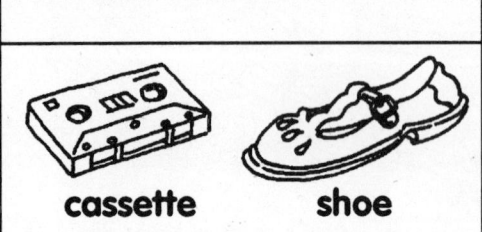

cassette   shoe

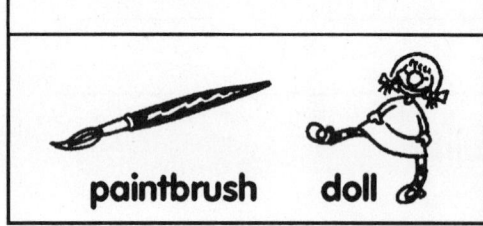

paintbrush   doll

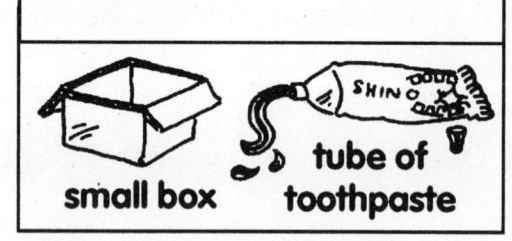

small box   tube of toothpaste

♣ Now try some of your own.

Name _____

Mass

Seesaw

You will need: a seesaw, a pencil.

♣ Work in a small group.

♣ Use a seesaw to compare the weights of some of the people in your group.

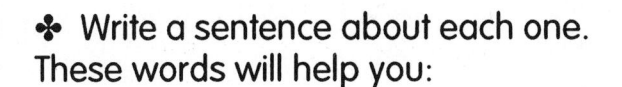

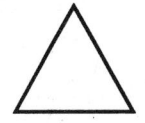

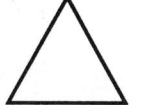

♣ Draw what happened on the seesaws below.

♣ Write a sentence about each one.
These words will help you:

Megan heavier

Victoria lighter

Megan is heavier than Victoria.

| heavier | lighter | same weight |

Teacher Timesavers: Measurement skills

Mass

Blocks

Name _____

Blocks

You will need: a balance, some blocks, a collection of small objects, a pencil.

♣ Put each object in turn on one end of the balance.

♣ Estimate how many blocks it will take to balance the object.

♣ Use blocks to check your estimate.

♣ Record your work on the scales below.

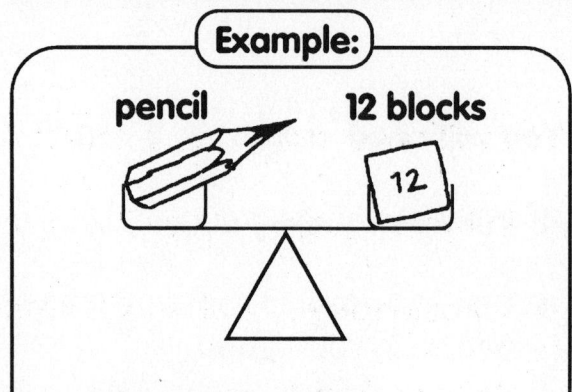

Example:

pencil   12 blocks

Estimate: 18 blocks
A pencil is
balanced by **12** blocks.

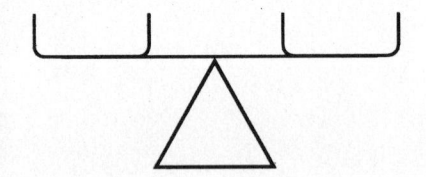

Estimate: ☐ blocks

A _____ is
balanced by ☐ blocks.

Estimate: ☐ blocks

A _____ is
balanced by ☐ blocks.

Estimate: ☐ blocks

A _____ is
balanced by ☐ blocks.

♣ Which object was the heaviest? _____

Which object was the lightest? _____

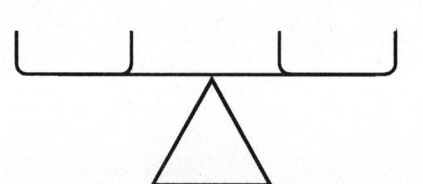

Name _____

Mass

My shoe

My shoe

You will need: a balance, a collection of small objects, a pencil.

♣ Put your shoe on one end of the balance.

♣ Try balancing your shoe with different objects in turn.

♣ Write or draw the objects which balance your shoe in the circles below.

My shoe is balanced by…

Teacher Timesavers: Measurement skills

Mass

Plasticine

Name _____

Plasticine

You will need: a balance, some Plasticine, a pencil, some shells (or marbles, LEGO or blocks).

♣ Put a lump of Plasticine on one end of the balance.

♣ Estimate how many shells it will take to balance it.

♣ Use shells to check your estimate.

♣ Record your work on the scales.

♣ Try this with lumps of Plasticine of different sizes.

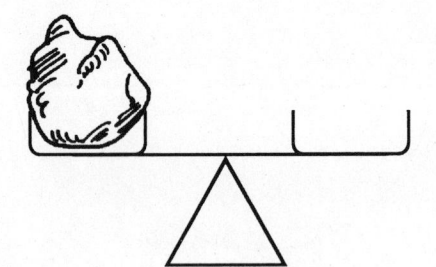

Estimate: _____

The Plasticine is balanced

by _____ .

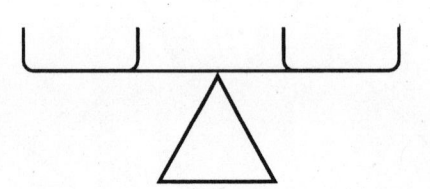

Estimate: _____

The Plasticine is balanced

by _____ .

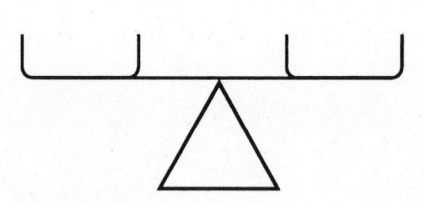

Estimate: _____

The Plasticine is balanced

by _____ .

Teacher Timesavers: Measurement skills

Name _____

Mass

Changing shape

Changing shape

You will need: a balance, Plasticine, some blocks, a pencil.

✤ Take a lump of Plasticine and make it into a ball shape.

✤ Weigh the Plasticine using some blocks.

✤ Record how many blocks it takes to balance the Plasticine in the first box.

✤ Now make the same lump of Plasticine into five different shapes in turn.

✤ Use blocks to weigh each shape.

✤ Record your work in the other boxes.

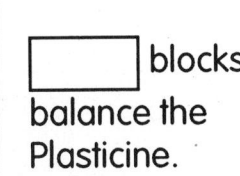

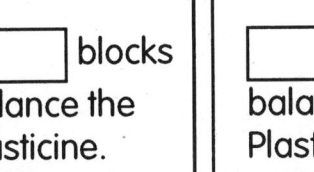

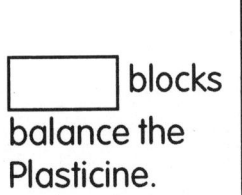

| ☐ blocks balance the Plasticine. | ☐ blocks balance the Plasticine. | ☐ blocks balance the Plasticine. | ☐ blocks balance the Plasticine. | ☐ blocks balance the Plasticine. | ☐ blocks balance the Plasticine. |

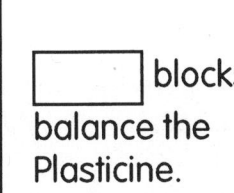

✤ Discuss your answers with a friend and write down what you have discovered.

_____

_____

Teacher Timesavers: Measurement skills

Mass
Kilograms

Name _____

Kilograms

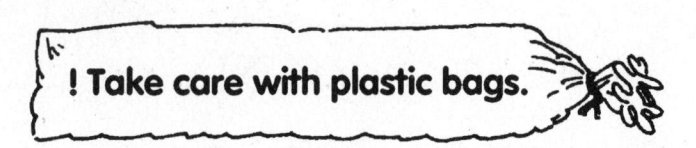

! Take care with plastic bags.

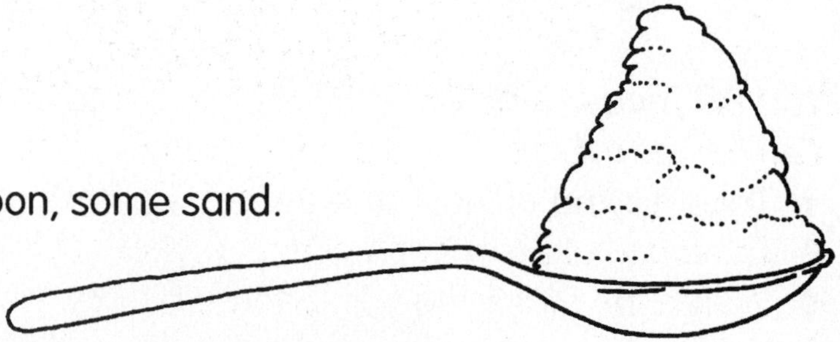

You will need: a 1kg weight, a balance, two plastic bags, a large spoon, some sand.

❖ Use the 1kg weight and the balance to measure out 1kg of sand.

❖ Put the sand in a plastic bag.

❖ Use the 1kg of sand and the balance to find:

Three objects that weigh about 1kg
1 _____
2 _____
3 _____

Three objects that weigh less than 1kg
1 _____
2 _____
3 _____

Three objects that weigh more than 1kg
1 _____
2 _____
3 _____

❖ Use your 1kg bag of sand and the balance to make a ½kg bag of sand.

❖ Explain what you did. _____
_____

❖ Use your ½kg bag of sand and the balance to find:

Three objects that weigh about ½kg
1 _____
2 _____
3 _____

Three objects that weigh less than ½kg
1 _____
2 _____
3 _____

Three objects that weigh more than ½kg
1 _____
2 _____
3 _____

Name _____

Mass

Predicting

Predicting

a level cup

You will need: a cup, a balance, weights, some water, some sand, some rice, some pasta, some rice crispies.

✤ Think about how much a level cup of each of the above substances will weigh.

✤ List them in order from lightest to heaviest.

My predictions 1 _____
2 _____
3 _____
4 _____
5 _____

lightest
↓
heaviest

1 _____
2 _____
3 _____
4 _____
5 _____

After weighing

✤ Now weigh a level cup of each substance to check your predictions.

✤ List them in order from lightest to heaviest.

✤ Were your predictions correct?

Explain. _____

✤ Which substance was the heaviest? _____

✤ Which substance was the lightest? _____

Substance	Weight
a cup of water	
a cup of sand	
a cup of rice	
a cup of pasta	
a cup of rice crispies	

Teacher Timesavers: Measurement skills

Mass
Smaller weights

Name _____

Smaller weights

You will need: a balance; a collection of small objects including a paperclip, a pencil, an eraser, a feather and a coin.

✤ Estimate how much each object weighs.

✤ Record your estimates in the table.

✤ Weigh each object.

✤ Record your results in the table.

✤ Choose five objects of your own and complete the table.

✤ Weigh out 20g of each of the following objects.

✤ Record how many objects make up 20g.

☐ coins weigh 20g   ☐ paperclips weigh 20g

☐ feathers weigh 20g   ☐ pencils weigh 20g

☐ erasers weigh 20g

✤ Why are the amounts different? _____

_____

Object	Estimated weight (g)	Actual weight (g)
a paperclip		
a pencil		
an eraser		
a feather		
a coin		

Name _____

Mass
Grams

Grams

1kg = 1000g

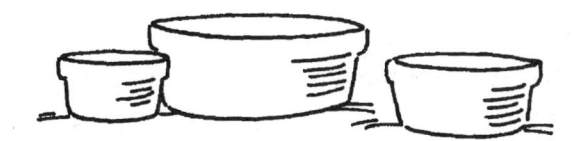

You will need: a balance, a collection of small objects, a pencil.

✤ Make a list of ten small objects in the table.

✤ Estimate the weight, in grams, of each object.

✤ Weigh each object in grams.

✤ Convert your answers to kilograms (and grams).

✤ List the objects in order from lightest to heaviest.

lightest ↓ **heaviest**

Object	Estimated weight (g)	Actual weight (g)	Actual weight (kg)

Teacher Timesavers: Measurement skills

Mass

Gifts

Gifts

Available weights: 500g, 200g, 100g, 50g, 20g, 10g, 5g, 1g

✤ Which of these weights would you use to balance each of the gift boxes below?

Draw the weights.

For example: 225g = 200g + 20g + 5g

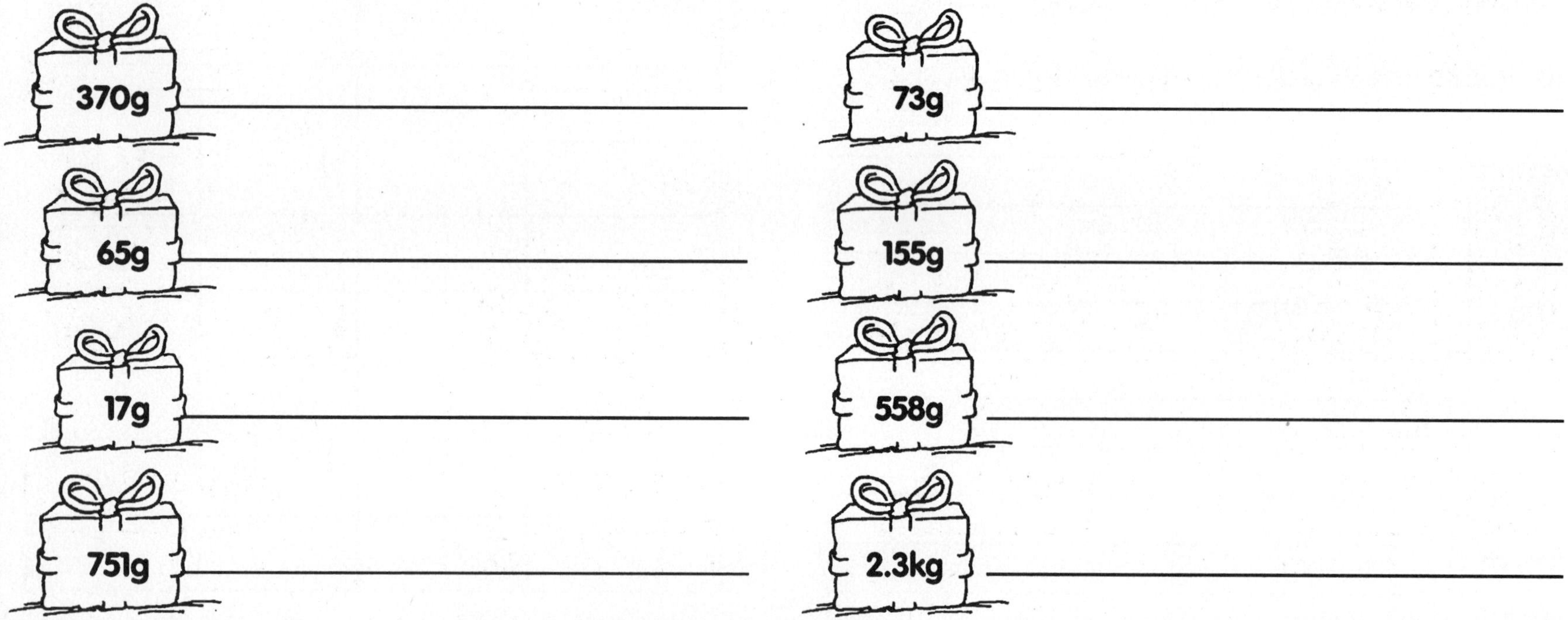

- 370g _____
- 65g _____
- 17g _____
- 751g _____
- 73g _____
- 155g _____
- 558g _____
- 2.3kg _____

Name _____

Mass
Find the weight

Find the weight

♣ Find the weight of each box.
The first one has been done for you.

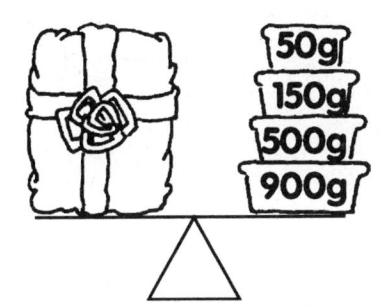

Box 1 — Weights: 50g, 150g, 500g, 900g
Weight of box
= 1600g
= 1.6kg

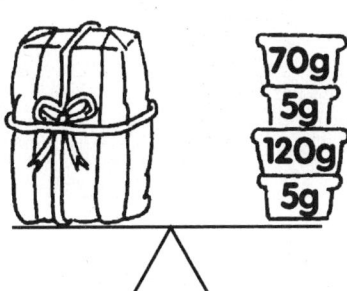

Box 2 — Weights: 70g, 5g, 120g, 5g
Weight of box
= _____ g
= _____ kg

Box 3 — Weights: 200g, 250g, 100g
Weight of box
= _____ g
= _____ kg

Box 4 — Weights: 200g, 600g, 10g
Weight of box
= _____ g
= _____ kg

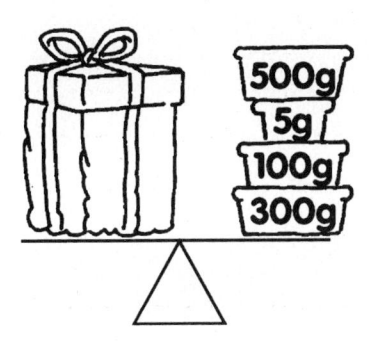

Box 5 — Weights: 500g, 5g, 100g, 300g
Weight of box
= _____ g
= _____ kg

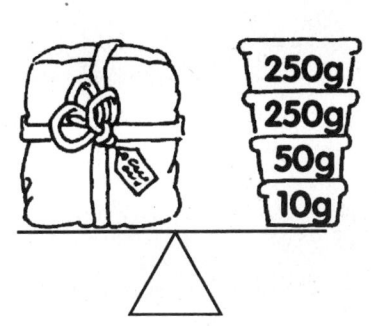

Box 6 — Weights: 250g, 250g, 50g, 10g
Weight of box
= _____ g
= _____ kg

Box 7 — Weights: 100g, 40g, 800g, 90g
Weight of box
= _____ g
= _____ kg

Box 8 — Weights: 60g, 80g, 500g, 100g, 500g
Weight of box
= _____ g
= _____ kg

Teacher Timesavers: Measurement skills

Mass

Tins and packets

Name _____

Tins and packets

You will need: a pencil, scissors, paper, paste, a collection of empty tins and packets.

✣ Find ten labels or packets that state the weight of the contents.

✣ In each box, record the name of the food item and its weight.

✣ Cut out the boxes and place the food items in order from lightest to heaviest.

✣ Paste them on a sheet of paper.

Cut

✣ Was the largest package the heaviest? _____

✣ Was the smallest package the lightest? _____

Name _____

Mass

Grams, kilograms or tonnes?

Grams, kilograms or tonnes?

1000g = 1kg
1000kg = 1 tonne

✤ Which unit would you use to measure each of these?
List the things in the correct boxes.

Grams (g)	Kilograms (kg)	Tonnes

✤ Add another item to each box.

a £1 coin	a caterpillar
an elephant	a feather
a hat	a boy
a frog	a car
a hippopotamus	a tennis racquet
a golf ball	a baby
a train	an aeroplane
a sweet	a fridge

Teacher Timesavers: Measurement skills

Mass

Throw the ball

Name _____

Throw the ball

You will need: a pencil, a balance, a metre ruler, all the balls listed below.

♣ Weigh each of the balls.

♣ Record your answers in the table.

♣ Use this information to predict:
- Which ball will you be able to throw the furthest? _____ Why? _____
- Which ball will you be able to throw the least distance? _____ Why? _____

Type of ball	Weight (g)	Distance thrown (m)
a balloon		
a shot		
a golf ball		
a tennis ball		
a table tennis ball		
a netball		
a football		
a squash ball		

♣ Throw each ball and record in the table the distance it travelled.

♣ Were your predictions correct?

_____

_____

♣ What other factors could have affected the length of throw?

_____

_____

50

Teacher Timesavers: Measurement skills

Name _____

Mass

Estimating more than one

Estimating more than one

You will need: ten of each of the objects listed in the table, a balance, weights.

✤ Weigh one pencil.

✤ Predict the weight of ten pencils.

✤ Weigh the ten pencils to check your prediction.

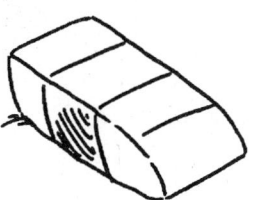

✤ Record your results in the table as you go along.

✤ Repeat this procedure with the other objects.

✤ Try this with three more objects and complete the table.

Objects	Weight of one (g)	Predicted weight of ten (g)	Actual weight of ten (g)
pencils			
erasers			
blocks			
rulers			
playing cards			

✤ If you know the weight of one object, explain how you can easily find the weight of ten.

_____

_____

_____

Teacher Timesavers: Measurement skills

Mass

Weighing ourselves

You will need: a set of bathroom scales, a calculator, a pencil.

♣ Use the bathroom scales to weigh all the members of your class. Record the results in the table.

Boys	Weight (kg)	Girls	Weight (kg)
Total			**Total**

♣ Use a calculator to work out:
- the total weight of the boys
- the total weight of the girls
- the total weight of the class
- the average weight of the boys
- the average weight of the girls

♣ How do the average weights compare? _____

♣ Would an older class have the same average weights? _____

Explain. _____

52   Teacher Timesavers: Measurement skills

Name _____

Mass

Muffins

Muffins

✤ Use the scales below to convert the quantities in the muffin recipe to metric measures.

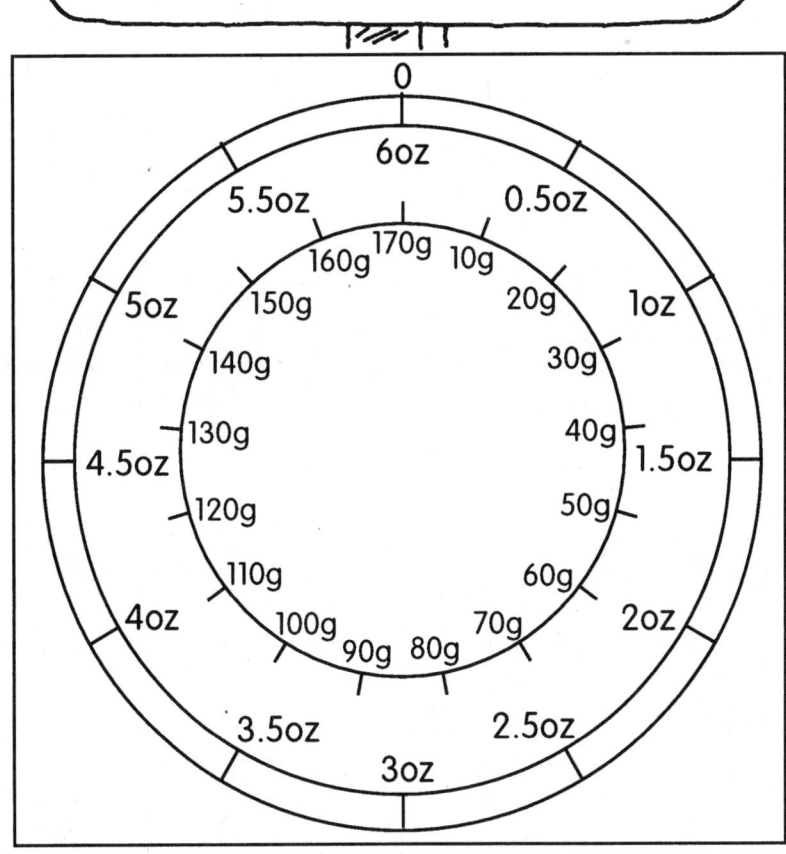

Basic muffin mixture

5oz plain flour _____
1½oz caster sugar _____
2oz butter _____
4fl oz milk _____
½ teaspoon baking powder _____
¼ teaspoon salt _____
½ teaspoon vanilla essence _____

For blueberry and pecan muffins, add:

4oz small blueberries _____
2oz pecan nuts _____

For apricot and pecan muffins, add:

4oz fresh apricots _____
1oz pecan nuts _____
3oz icing sugar _____
½ teaspoon cinnamon powder _____

Teacher Timesavers: Measurement skills

Mass

Wet and dry

Wet and dry

You will need: a bowl of water, a balance, weights, a pencil, the objects listed in the table.

✤ Weigh each of the objects.

✤ Record your results in the table.

✤ Soak each object in water and weigh it again.

✤ Record your results.

✤ Calculate the difference between the wet and the dry weights.

✤ How did the wet and the dry weights differ?

_____

_____

✤ Was it the same for all the objects? Explain.

_____

_____

Object	Dry weight (g)	Wet weight (g)	Difference between wet and dry weights (g)
a sponge			
a pencil			
a hand towel			
a ruler			
a handkerchief			
a cup			
a paper towel			
a sock			

Teacher Timesavers: Measurement skills

Name _____

Mass

Net weight/gross weight

Net weight/gross weight

Net weight = weight of contents only (excludes weight of package/container)

Gross weight = total weight (includes weight of package/container)

You will need: two containers, a balance, weights, some sand, a pencil.

✤ Weigh one container.

✤ Now fill the container with sand and weigh it again.

✤ Use this information to work out how much the sand weighs.

✤ Weigh the sand to see if your calculation was correct.

✤ Write all your answers in the table below.

Weight of container		
Weight of container + sand (gross weight)		
Calculated weight of sand (net weight)		
Measured weight of sand (net weight)		

✤ Repeat this procedure using the second container.

✤ Write your answers on the back of this sheet.

✤ Complete the table below.

Weight of container	Net weight	Gross weight
320g	240g	
	475g	525g
1.8kg	2.7kg	
40g		150g
	32kg	47.5kg

Teacher Timesavers: Measurement skills

Capacity and volume

Name _____

Full or empty?

Full or empty?

You will need: some old magazines, a pencil.

✤ Look at this picture.

✤ Draw a cross (**X**) on each container that is empty.

✤ Draw a circle (**O**) round each container that is full.

✤ Look through a magazine to find some 'full'/'empty' pictures.

Name _____

Capacity and volume

Half-full

Half-full

You will need: scissors, paste, a pencil.

♣ Look at each of the pictures on the right and decide whether the container shown is full, half-full or empty.

♣ Cut out each picture and paste it in the correct box.

Cut

Full	Empty	Half-full

♣ Draw another picture to go in each box.

Teacher Timesavers: Measurement skills

57

Capacity and volume

Name _____

Which holds most?

Which holds most?

You will need: three different empty containers, some sand, a pencil, scissors, paper, sticky tape.

♣ Label the containers **A**, **B** and **C**.

♣ Draw them in these boxes.

♣ Which container do you think will hold the most?

♣ Which container do you think will hold the least?

♣ Do you think any of them will hold the same amount?

_____

♣ Check your predictions by pouring.

♣ Draw the containers again, this time in order, starting with the container which holds the least.

A   B   C

least   most

58   Teacher Timesavers: Measurement skills

Name _____

Capacity and volume
Cupfuls

Cupfuls

You will need: six different empty containers, a cup, a pencil, scissors, paper, sticky tape.

✤ Label the containers **A**, **B**, **C**, **D**, **E** and **F**.

✤ Draw them in these boxes.

✤ Guess, then measure, how many cupfuls of water each of the containers will hold.

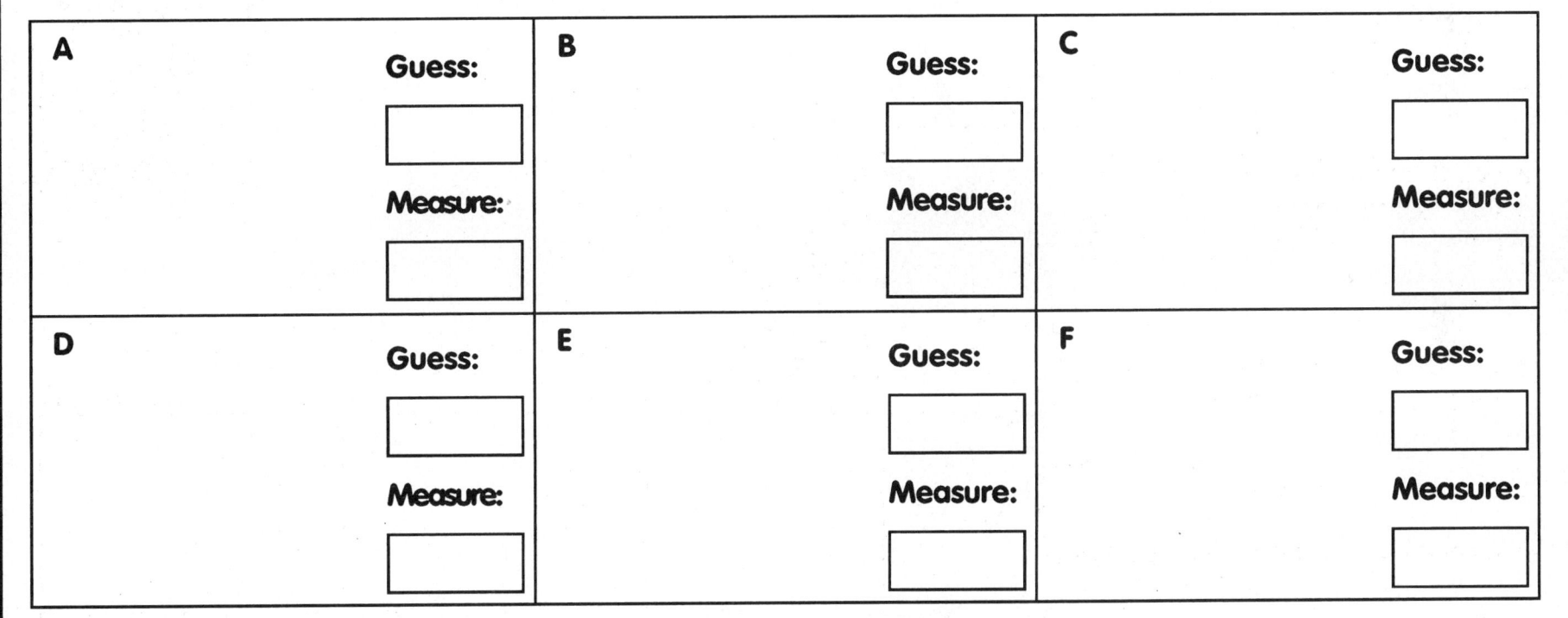

A	B	C
Guess: Measure:	Guess: Measure:	Guess: Measure:
D Guess: Measure:	**E** Guess: Measure:	**F** Guess: Measure:

✤ List the containers in order from smallest capacity to largest capacity.

Teacher Timesavers: Measurement skills

59

Capacity and volume

How many?

Name _____

How many?

You will need: a collection of empty containers, a pencil.

♣ Choose one big container.

♣ Draw it in the big square.

♣ In turn, use some other smaller containers to fill the big container with water.

♣ For each small container you try, draw a picture and complete a sentence.

This container has to be filled ☐ times in order to fill this one.

This container has to be filled ☐ times in order to fill this one.

This container has to be filled ☐ times in order to fill this one.

This container has to be filled ☐ times in order to fill this one.

This container has to be filled ☐ times in order to fill this one.

60

Teacher Timesavers: Measurement skills

Name _____

Capacity and volume

New paint

New paint

You will need: a pencil, paper, a mixing bowl, a wooden spoon, an eggcup, all the ingredients listed below.

♣ Make up a 'recipe' for a new type of paint.

- You can use only the ingredients listed below.
- You must measure them out with an eggcup.
- You can use only ten eggcupfuls altogether.

Ingredients
water
powder paint (blue, yellow, red)
flour
liquid paint (blue, yellow, red)
soap powder
coloured water

♣ Make the paint and try to paint with it. Was it successful?

Why?/Why not? _____

_____

My paint recipe

Teacher Timesavers: Measurement skills

Capacity and volume
Litres

Name _____

Litres

You will need: a large empty bottle, some other empty containers, a 1l jug, paper, sticky tape, scissors, a pencil.

✤ Cut out a strip of paper and tape it to the large bottle.

✤ Using the 1l jug, pour 1l of water into the bottle.

✤ Mark the level on the paper strip.

✤ Repeat this procedure until the bottle is full.

✤ Use your litre measure to find the capacity of several other containers.

✤ Record your estimate of the capacity of each one first.

Container	Estimated capacity (l)	Actual capacity (l)

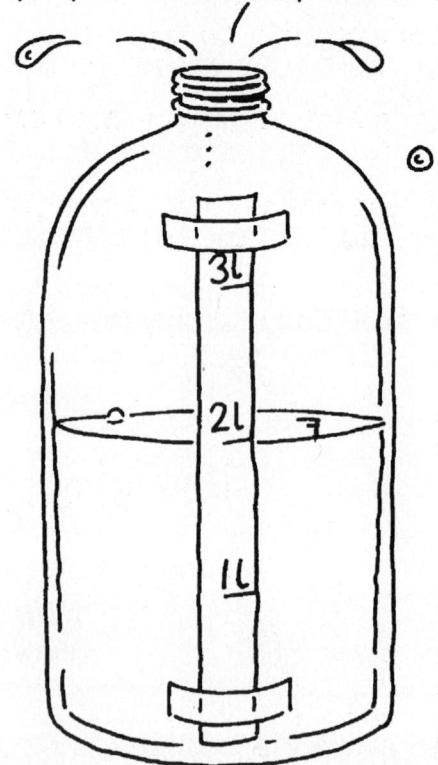

These words will help you:
a bit more than
a bit less than
about halfway between
about equal to

Name _____

Capacity and volume
Make a litre

Make a litre

You will need: a pencil, a 1l container, five smaller containers (for example, an eggcup, a plastic cup, a pill bottle, a yoghurt pot).

♣ In turn, use each small container to fill the 1l container.

♣ Draw how many times you had to fill the small container.

♣ Which of the small containers was the easiest to use? _____ Why? _____

♣ If you had to fill a 5l container, which of the small containers would you use? _____ Why? _____

Teacher Timesavers: Measurement skills

Capacity and volume

Name _____

More or less?

More or less?

You will need: scissors, paste.

✤ Look at the pictures.

✤ How much water do you think each container would hold?

✤ Cut out the pictures and paste them in the correct boxes.

Cut

About 1l	Less than 1l	More than 1l

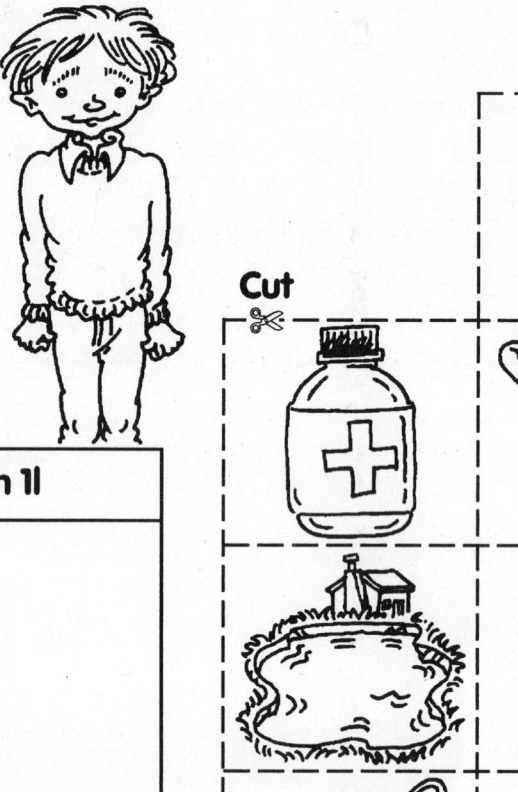

64

Teacher Timesavers: Measurement skills

Name _____

Capacity and volume

Halves and quarters

Halves and quarters

You will need: a 1l jug, six different empty containers, scissors, sticky tape, paper, a pencil.

♣ Label the containers **A, B, C, D, E** and **F**.

♣ Using the 1l jug, work out how much water each container will hold.

♣ Write the letters **A–F** in the correct boxes.

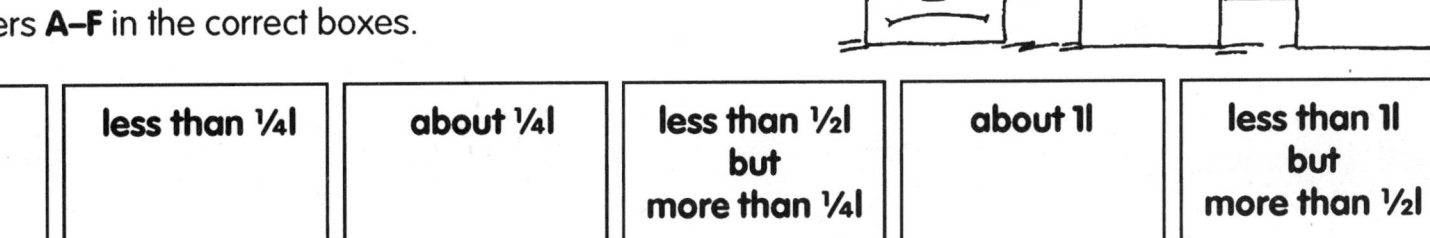

about ½l	less than ¼l	about ¼l	less than ½l but more than ¼l	about 1l	less than 1l but more than ½l

♣ Look at these pictures.

1. Milk ¼l
2. ¼l
3. ½l
4. ¾l iZZ
5. ½l Juice
6. ¼l Beer

♣ Which containers put together would make more than 1l? _____

_____

_____

_____

_____

Teacher Timesavers: Measurement skills

65

Capacity and volume
Spoons

Spoons

You will need: a collection of different spoons, a measuring cylinder, a pencil.

✤ Choose six spoons.

✤ Try to put them in order, starting with the one with the smallest capacity.

✤ Draw them here.

← **smallest capacity**   **largest capacity** →

            1   2   3   4   5   6

✤ Use a measuring cylinder to measure the capacity of each spoon.

✤ Record your results in this table.

Spoon	Capacity

✤ Did you have the spoons in the correct order? _____

Explain. _____

_____

_____

✤ Do all spoons of the same type (tablespoon, teaspoon, etc.) have the same capacity?
Conduct a test to check your ideas.

Name _____

Capacity and volume
Evaporation

Evaporation

You will need: three containers shaped like these: a measuring cylinder, a pencil, scissors, paper, sticky tape.

♣ Label the containers **A, B** and **C**.

♣ Place the same amount of water in each container.

♣ Leave them for a few days.

♣ Measure the amount of water that is left.

♣ Record your results in the table.

♣ Which container lost the most water? ☐

♣ Which container lost the least amount of water? ☐

Why? _____

♣ Look at these pictures.
Draw circles round the containers which would not lose much water through evaporation.

Container	Amount of water I put in	Amount of water left	Amount of water lost during evaporation
A			
B			
C			

Teacher Timesavers: Measurement skills

Capacity and volume

Reading a scale 1

You will need: coloured pencils.

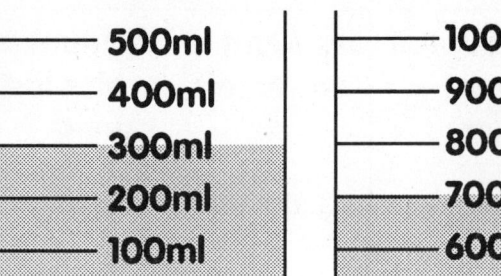

✤ What is the volume of liquid in each of these jars?

Volume = _____   Volume = _____   Volume = _____   Volume = _____   Volume = _____

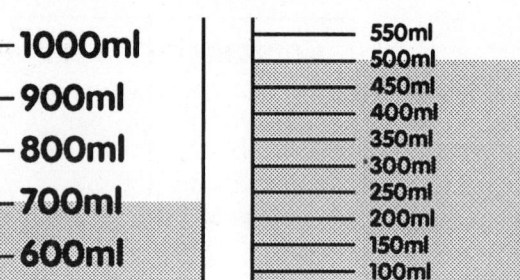

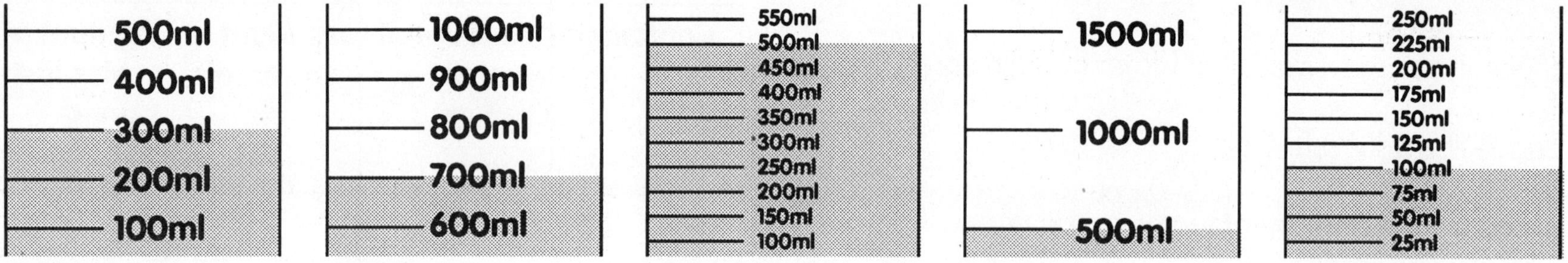

✤ Complete the scales below.

✤ Colour each jar to the level required to show the correct volume.

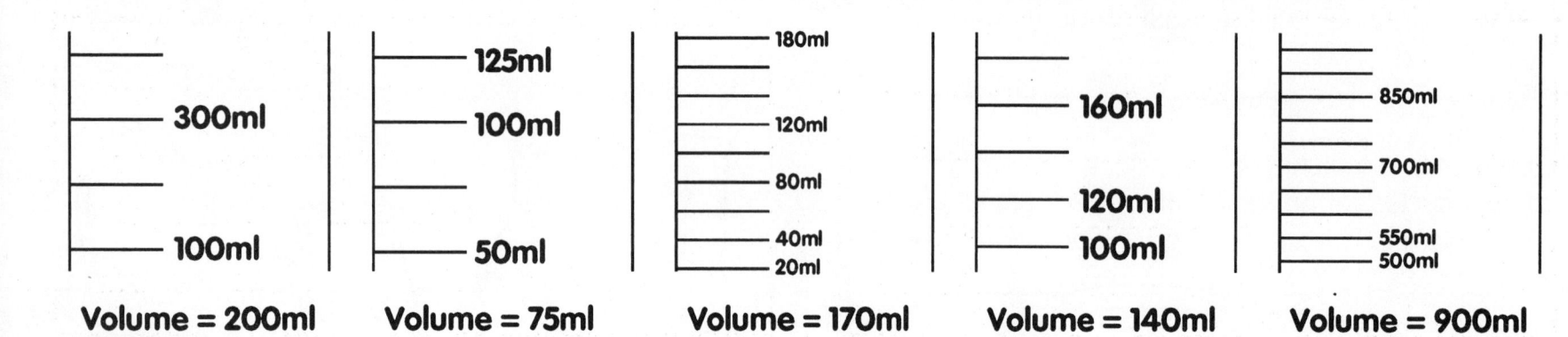

Volume = 200ml   Volume = 75ml   Volume = 170ml   Volume = 140ml   Volume = 900ml

68 Teacher Timesavers: Measurement skills

Name _____

Capacity and volume

Reading a scale 2

Reading a scale 2

You will need: a pencil, a collection of containers with measuring scales.

✤ Estimate the volume in each of these jars.

500ml	2000ml	225ml	100ml	370ml
400ml	1500ml	200ml	80ml	360ml
300ml	1000ml	175ml	60ml	350ml
200ml	500ml	150ml	40ml	340ml
100ml		125ml	20ml	330ml

Volume = _____   Volume = _____   Volume = _____   Volume = _____   Volume = _____

✤ Choose two of the containers used to measure volume.

✤ Draw their scales and explain what they mean.

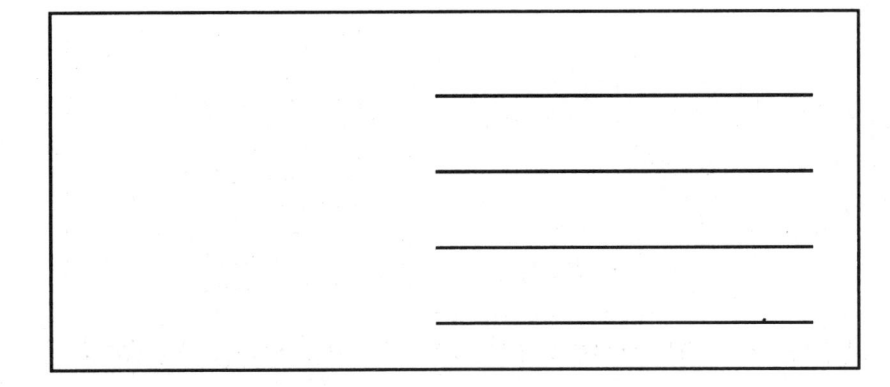

Teacher Timesavers: Measurement skills

69

Capacity and volume

Name _____

Litres and millilitres

Litres and millilitres

This shopkeeper has decided that all the liquid goods in his shop must be labelled in litres.

♣ Change all the labels for him.

- Milk 500ml
- Mayo 200ml
- pop 2250ml
- Juice 1200ml
- Vinegar 1000ml
- Oil 1500ml
- 250ml

This shopkeeper has decided that all the liquid goods in her shop must be labelled in millilitres.

♣ Change all the labels for her.

- Beer ¼ l
- Wine ½ l
- Soap 0.5l
- 1l
- 0.1l
- dowlene 2.5l
- Hand lotion 0.2l

♣ How would you label liquids like these? _____ Why? _____

Teacher Timesavers: Measurement skills

Name _____

Capacity and volume
Cooking

Cooking

Many recipes use Imperial measures only.

♣ Use the information in the conversion chart to rewrite the recipe using metric units.

Debra's Delicious Punch

1 pint pineapple juice
½ pint orange juice
½ pint lemonade
¾ pint ginger ale
2fl oz lemon juice
¼ pint water (frozen into ice cubes)

Conversion chart	
2fl oz	55ml
3fl oz	75ml
¼ pint	150ml
½ pint	275ml
¾ pint	425ml
1 pint	570ml
1¼ pints	725ml
1¾ pints	1l
2 pints	1.2l

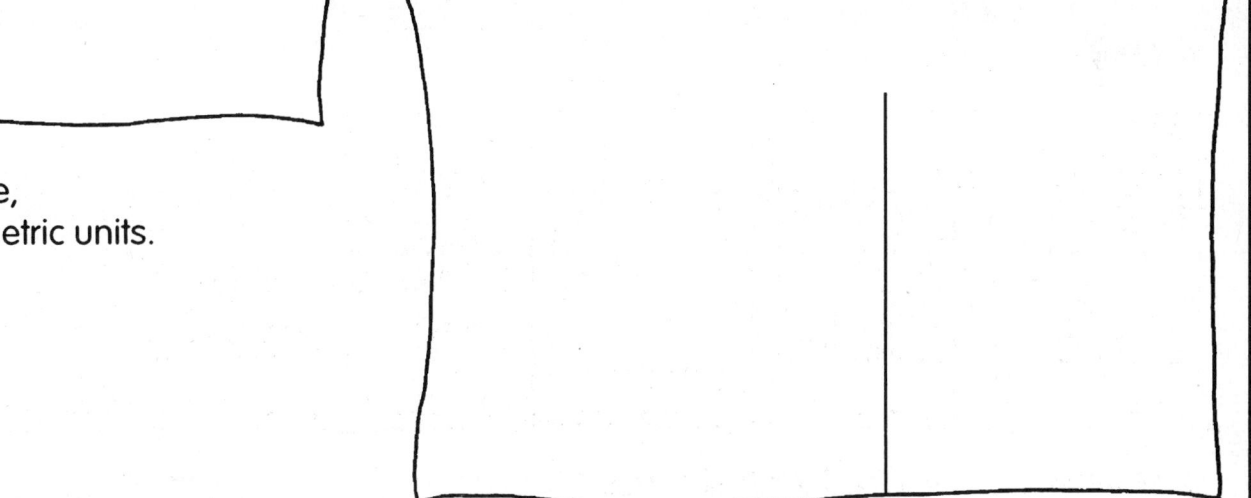

♣ Make up your own punch recipe, writing it in both Imperial and metric units.

Teacher Timesavers: Measurement skills

Capacity and volume

Pints and gallons

Name _____

Pints and gallons

A game for two or more players

You will need: scissors.

A gallon is an Imperial measure of capacity. One gallon is equal to eight pints.

1 gallon = 8 pints

- Cut out the cards below.
- Put them into two groups, gallons and pints.
- In turn, choose a card from each group.
- If they match, keep them and have another turn.
- If they don't match, the next player has a turn.
- The winner is the player with the most pairs when all the cards have been used up.

♣ Think of some things which are still measured in either pints or gallons. List them on the back of this sheet.

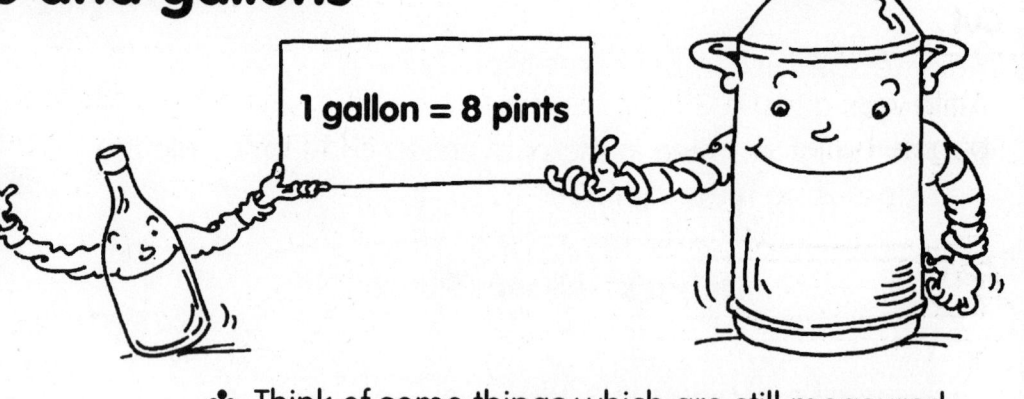

Cut

1 gallon	2½ gallons	7 gallons	½ gallon	4 gallons	40 pints
24 pints	100 gallons	8 pints	¼ gallon	20 pints	3 gallons
800 pints	10 gallons	2 gallons	5 gallons	56 pints	32 pints
4 pints	72 gallons	576 pints	16 pints	2 pints	80 pints

Name _____

Capacity and volume

Volume problems (cards)

Volume problems (cards)

Cut

Attila was given a 900ml bottle of bubble bath.

♣ If he uses 15ml for each bath, how many bubble baths can he have?

Louisa and Heidi want to make a fruit punch. They are going to use 1.5l of lemonade, 900ml of cola and 500ml of orange juice.

♣ Will the punch fit in their 2.5l punchbowl?

Sarah has a bad cold and needs to take 10ml of medicine three times a day for five days.

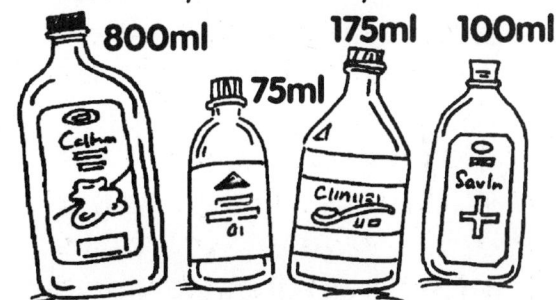

800ml 75ml 175ml 100ml

♣ Which size bottle of medicine will she need to buy?

♣ How many 750ml bottles of wine could be filled from a 15l barrel?

The Walters family buy 2l of milk every day.

♣ Work out how much each person drinks if:
  Mum drinks a quarter of it.
• Morgan drinks a quarter of it.
• Greg drinks half of it.

Jan-Henrik's petrol tank holds 28l. It is a quarter full.

♣ How much petrol does he have?

Teacher Timesavers: Measurement skills

Capacity and volume

Boxes

Boxes

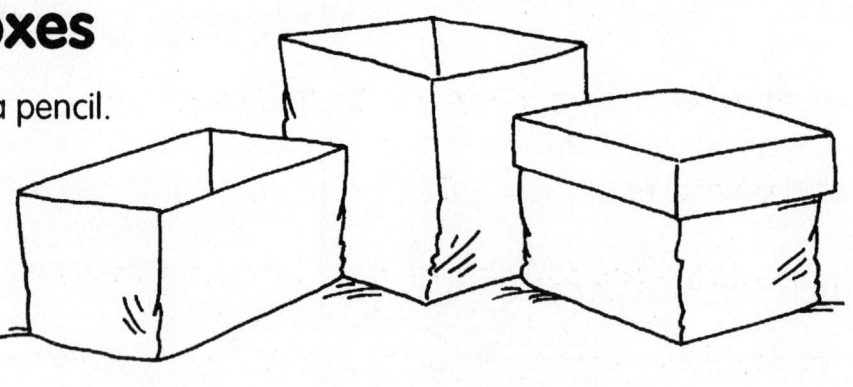

You will need: a collection of empty boxes, centicubes, a pencil.

♣ Choose four boxes.

♣ Label them **A**, **B**, **C** and **D**.

♣ Fill each box with cubes. They must fit edge to edge.

♣ Record how many cubes it took to fill each box.

The number of cubes that fit in a box shows you the volume of the box.

♣ Which box has the greatest volume? ☐

♣ Which box has the smallest volume? ☐

Box	Number of cubes
A	
B	
C	
D	

♣ Why do we use cubes rather than spheres or cylinders to measure volume?

_____

_____

♣ What sort of cubes would you need to measure the volume of a big box?

_____

_____

Name _____

Capacity and volume

Lids

Lids

You will need: a marker pen, a collection of lids, a measuring cylinder marked in millilitres.

✤ Label ten of the lids **A** to **J**.

✤ Estimate the capacity of each one and record your estimate in the table.

✤ Measure the capacity of each one with the measuring cylinder and record your result in the table.

Lid	Estimated capacity (ml)	Actual capacity (ml)
A		
B		
C		
D		
E		
F		
G		
H		
I		
J		

✤ Did any of the lids hold more than 100ml?
If so, which ones?

_____

_____

✤ Did any of the lids hold less than 10ml?
If so, which ones?

_____

_____

Teacher Timesavers: Measurement skills

Capacity and volume

In the shops

Name _____

In the shops

You will need: a collection of cartons, tins and bottles (or their labels) which have held liquids; scissors, a pencil.

♣ Choose ten of the packages (or labels).

♣ In each of the rectangles below, record the name of one of the items and its volume.

♣ Cut out the rectangles and place them in order, starting with the smallest volume.

♣ Did any of the containers hold the same volume? _____

Were they the same shape? _____

Cut ✂

76

Teacher Timesavers: Measurement skills

Capacity and volume

Name _____

Cubes

Cubes

You will need: interlocking cubes such as Multilink or Unifix, a pencil.

✤ Draw lines to show all the cubes within each outline.

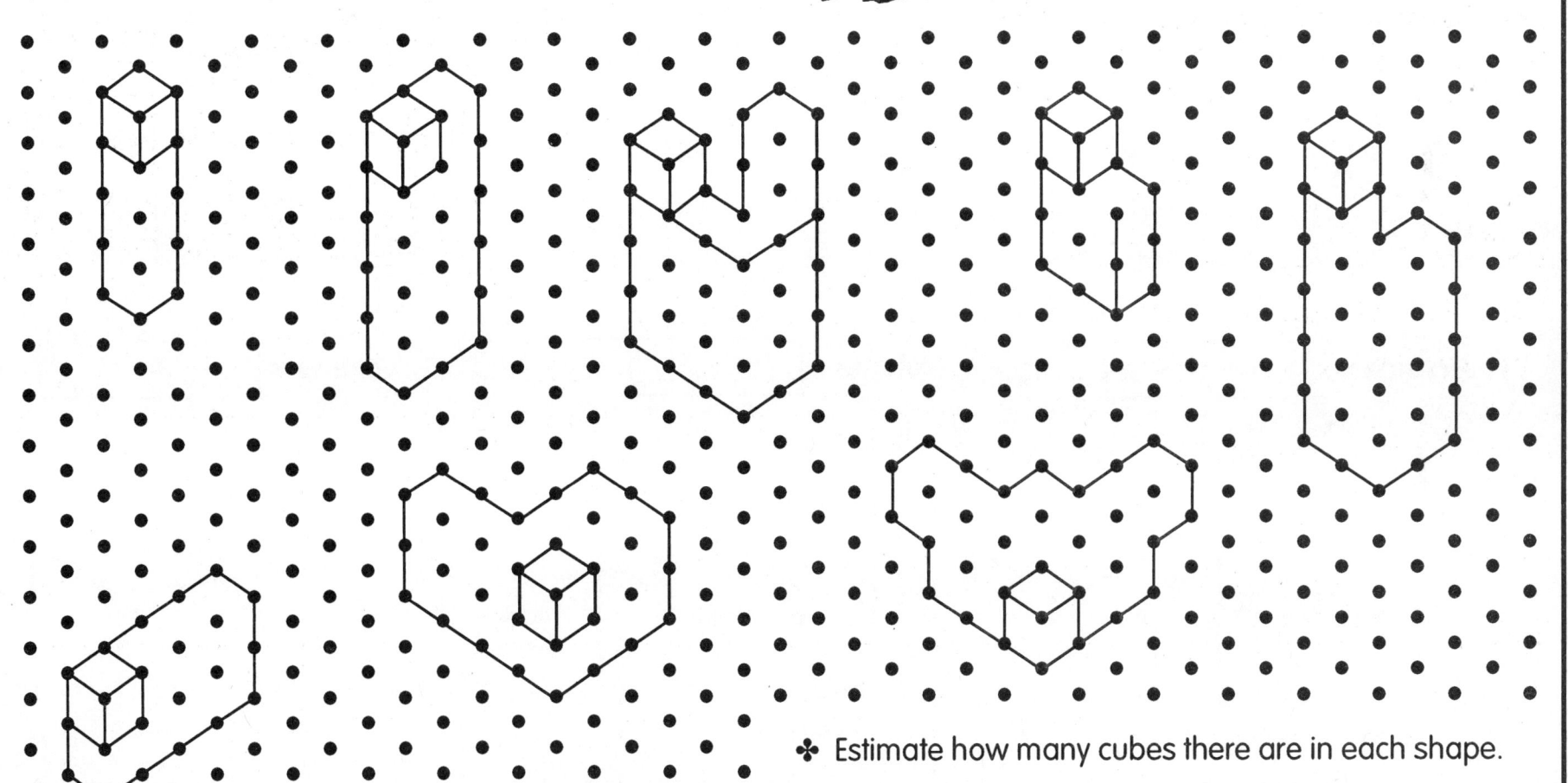

✤ Estimate how many cubes there are in each shape.

✤ Then make each shape to test your prediction.

Teacher Timesavers: Measurement skills

77

Capacity and volume

Cubes and cuboids

Name _____

Cubes and cuboids

Volume = length × breadth × height

✣ Calculate the volume of each shape in cubic centimetres (cm³).

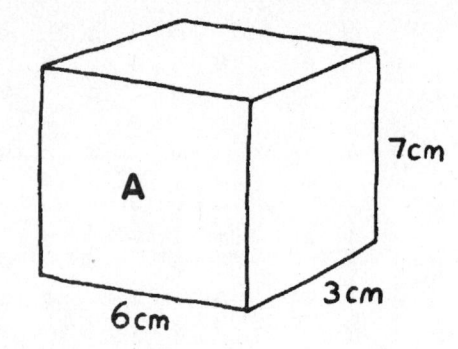

A — 6cm × 3cm × 7cm

Volume = _____

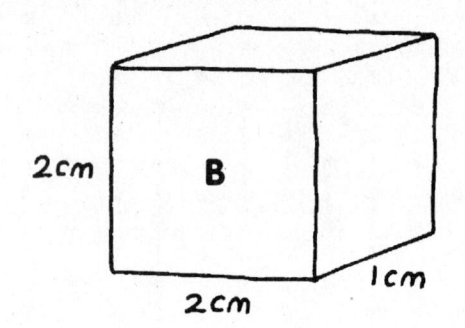

B — 2cm × 2cm × 1cm

Volume = _____

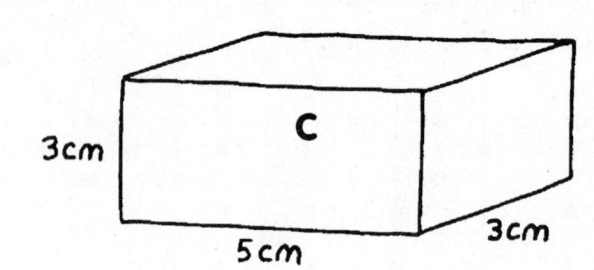

C — 5cm × 3cm × 3cm

Volume = _____

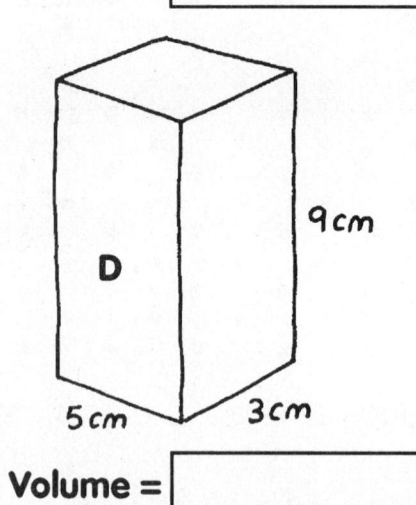

D — 5cm × 3cm × 9cm

Volume = _____

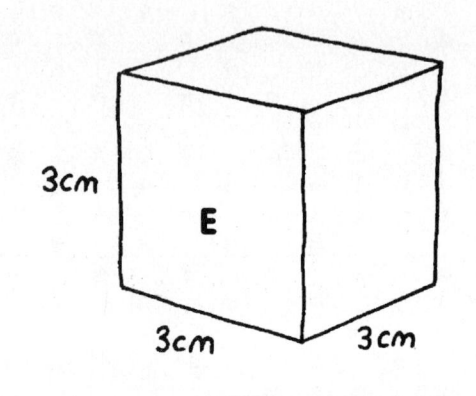

E — 3cm × 3cm × 3cm

Volume = _____

F — 12cm × 3cm × 4cm

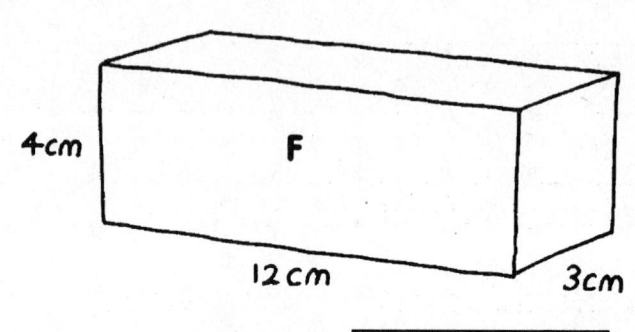

Volume = _____

78

Teacher Timesavers: Measurement skills

Name _____

Capacity and volume

Capacity and volume

You will need: a pencil, card, scissors, a centimetre ruler, sticky tape, sand, a measuring cylinder, centicubes.

♣ Working in a small group, make four cardboard cubes or cuboids of different sizes, using measurements in centimetres. It is easiest to draw a net first. Leave one side open.

♣ Label your boxes **A**, **B**, **C** and **D**.

♣ Use centicubes to find the volume of each box.

♣ Record your answers in the table.

net of a cube

Box	Volume in cubic centimetres (cm³)	Capacity in millilitres (ml)
A		
B		
C		
D		

net of a cuboid

♣ Use sand and a measuring cylinder to find the capacity of each box.

♣ Record your answers in the table.

♣ What did you discover? _____

Teacher Timesavers: Measurement skills

Time

Night and day

Name _____

Night and day

You will need: scissors.

♣ Look at these pictures. Do they show night or day?

♣ Cut out the pictures.

♣ Sort them into two sets: 'Night' and 'Day'.

Cut

80

Teacher Timesavers: Measurement skills

Name _____

Time
After school

After school

You will need: scissors, paste.

The pictures at the bottom of the sheet show some of the things you might do after school.

♣ Think about the order in which you would do them.

♣ Cut out the pictures.

♣ Paste them here in the correct order.

Paste 1	**Paste 2**	**Paste 3**	**Paste 4**

✂ Cut

Teacher Timesavers: Measurement skills

81

Time
O'clock

Name _____

O'clock

A game for two or more players

You will need: scissors.

- Cut out the cards.
- Place the cards face down.
- Each player in turn turns up two cards.
- If they match, the player keeps them and has another turn.
- If not, turn them back face down and it is the next player's turn.
- The winner is the player with the most pairs when all the cards have been used up.

Cut ✂

1 o'clock	2 o'clock	3 o'clock	4 o'clock	5 o'clock	6 o'clock
7 o'clock	8 o'clock	9 o'clock	10 o'clock	11 o'clock	12 o'clock

Teacher Timesavers: Measurement skills

Name _____

Time

Days of the week

Days of the week

You will need: a pencil, scissors, paste.

♣ Cut out the labels at the bottom of the page.
♣ Paste them into the small boxes in the correct order.

Paste	Paste	Paste	Paste	Paste	Paste	Paste

♣ In each of the large boxes, write down what you do on that day. For example:

Sunday	Monday
Visit Gran Watch TV	Go to school

♣ Which is your favourite day of the week? _____

Why? _____
_____

♣ Which day of the week do you like least? _____

Why? _____
_____

✂ Cut

Saturday	Thursday	Tuesday	Monday	Friday	Sunday	Wednesday

Teacher Timesavers: Measurement skills

Time
Making clocks

Name _____

Making clocks

You will need: a paper plate, a ruler, a split pin, scissors, coloured pencils.

✤ Use the paper plate, the split pin and the numbers and hands below to make a clock face. Decorate your clock in an interesting way before you add the hands.

This is a quick and easy way of positioning the numbers when making or drawing a clock.

- Cut out a large circle.
- Fold it in half and then in half again.
- Open it out and rule along the fold lines.
- Use the numbers **12**, **3**, **6** and **9** on the clock. The **12** goes at the top.
- Stick the other numbers on your clock face, spacing them evenly.

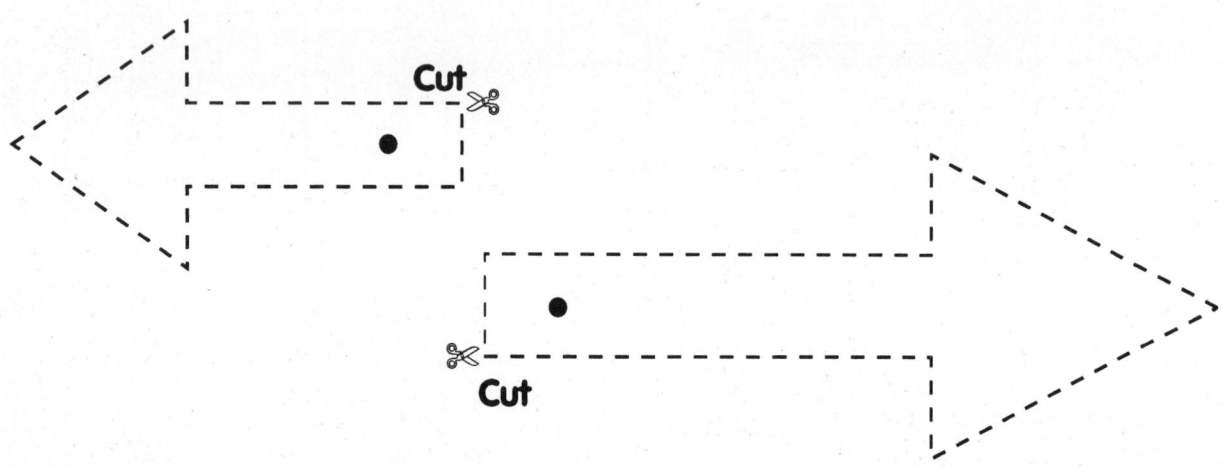

These don't look right.

Cut

Cut

1	2	3
4	5	6
7	8	9
10	11	12

Name _____

Time

The seasons

The seasons

You will need: paper, a ruler, a pencil, scissors, paste.

♣ On a large sheet of paper, draw four columns and label them like this:

Summer	Autumn	Winter	Spring

♣ Cut out the pictures below and paste each one in the correct column.

♣ Draw another picture in each column.

Cut

Teacher Timesavers: Measurement skills

Time

The calendar 1

Name _____

The calendar 1

You will need: scissors, coloured pencils, a hole-punch, a piece of string.

This is a project that you can add to each month.

♣ Cut out the calendar page on page 87.

♣ Write in the name of the month and the dates.
Remember to start on the correct day of the week.
This rhyme will help you to find out how many days there are in each month:

> Thirty days has September,
> April, June and November.
> All the rest have thirty-one.
> Not February – it's a different one.
> It has twenty-eight. That's fine!
> A leap year makes it twenty-nine.

♣ In the space below the name of the month, draw a picture or write a sentence about the month. For example, in December you may like to draw a Christmas picture.
♣ Complete the sentence at the bottom of the calendar page.
♣ Mark in any special days (holidays, birthdays, celebrations, special events).
♣ Make a front cover for your calendar.
You may like to include the rhyme above to help you throughout the year.
♣ Punch holes in your cover and first sheet and tie them together with a piece of string.
♣ Add another sheet each month until you have a complete calendar.

Teacher Timesavers: Measurement skills

Name _____

The calendar 2

Time

The calendar 2

Sunday	Monday	Tuesday	Wednesday	Thursday	Friday	Saturday

Cut

_____ has

_____ days.

Teacher Timesavers: Measurement skills

87

Time

BIRTHDAYS

Name _____

Birthdays

✤ On the back of this sheet, make a list of the children in your class.

✤ Next to each person's name, write down the month of his or her birthday. For example: Christopher – September.

✤ Record your information on the block graph below.

✤ Write down at least three things that your graph tells you.

Month	Number of children									
January										
February										
March										
April										
May										
June										
July										
August										
September										
October										
November										
December										

• _____

• _____

• _____

Teacher Timesavers: Measurement skills

Name _____

Time

Timing devices

Timing devices

You will need: the materials shown in one of the diagrams, a pencil.

♣ Make one of these timing devices:

Sand timer
⇐ funnel
⇐ sand
⇐ plastic container

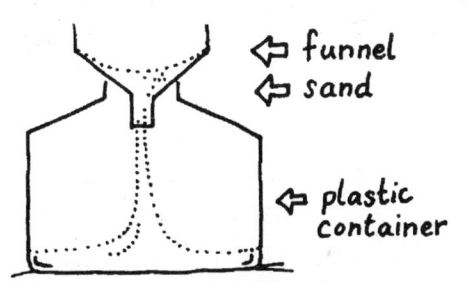

All the sand must trickle into the plastic container.

Water timer
⇐ water
⇐ cut off detergent bottle
⇐ plastic container

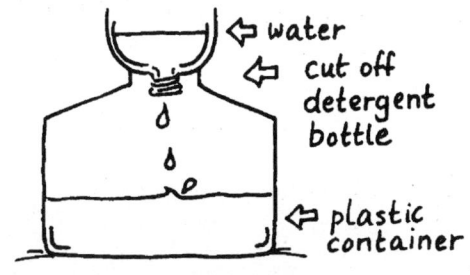

All the water must trickle into the plastic container.

Pendulum
⇐ tape
string ⇒
⇐ table
weight ⇒

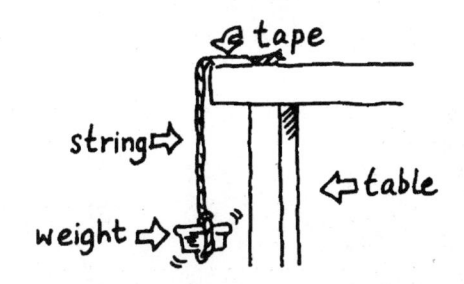

The pendulum must swing a certain number of times.

♣ Use your timing device to measure some different activities.
For example, how many jumps can you do?
How many times can you write your name?

♣ Write about each of the activities you completed. _____

_____

_____

♣ Invent and make another timing device.

Teacher Timesavers: Measurement skills

Time

Telling the time

Name _____

Telling the time

♣ Use the large clock to work out the times shown on the smaller clocks.

♣ Write the times under the clocks.

- o'clock — 12
- 5 minutes to — 11
- 5 minutes past — 1
- 10 minutes to — 10
- 10 minutes past — 2
- 15 minutes to or a quarter to — 9
- 15 minutes past or a quarter past — 3
- 20 minutes to — 8
- 20 minutes past — 4
- 25 minutes to — 7
- 25 minutes past — 5
- 30 minutes past or half-past — 6

90

Teacher Timesavers: Measurement skills

Name _____

Time

On time

On time

The display board on the right shows some of the train departure times from Central Station.

♣ As Station Master it is your job to complete the digital times next to the clocks and to answer the questions the passengers ask.

At what time does the train to Leeds leave?

The train to York is running two hours late. What time will it now leave?

It is 10:05. How long do I have to wait for the train to leave for Cardiff?

The trip to Edinburgh takes five hours. What time will the train arrive in Edinburgh?

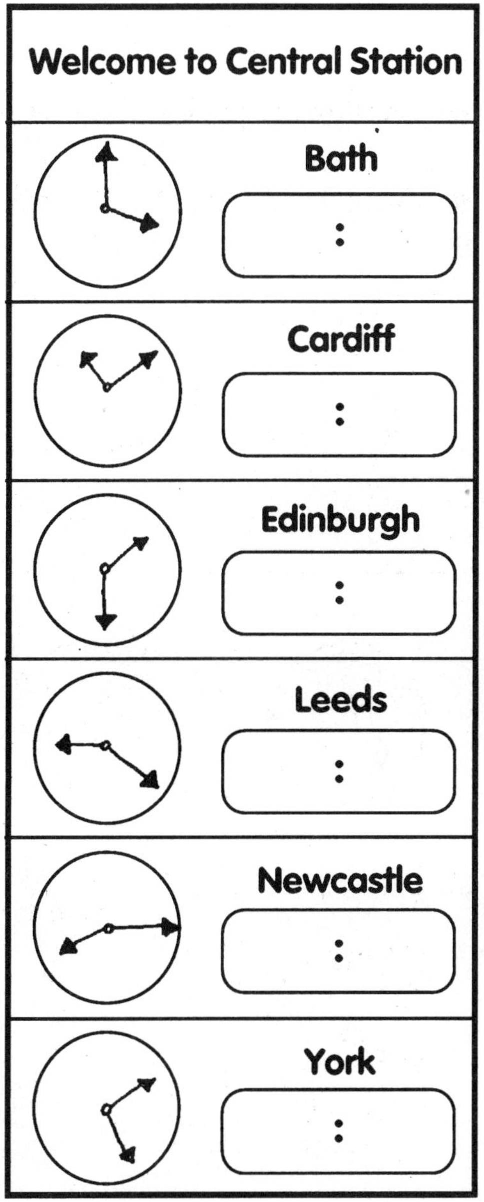

Welcome to Central Station

Clock	Destination	Digital
	Bath	:
	Cardiff	:
	Edinburgh	:
	Leeds	:
	Newcastle	:
	York	:

Teacher Timesavers: Measurement skills

91

Time
TV times

Name _____

TV times

You will need: a TV guide, a pencil.

✤ Using the TV guide, make a list of the programmes on BBC1 on a Monday night.

✤ Include the time each one starts.

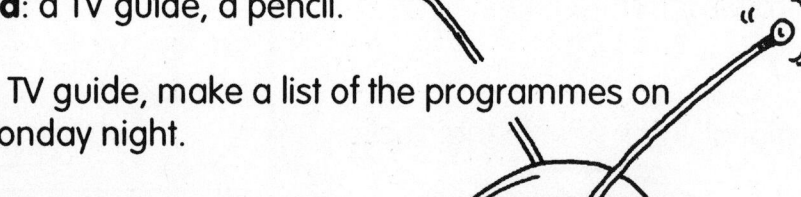

✤ Which programme is the longest?
_____

✤ Which programmes are 30 minutes long?
_____

✤ Is there a film?
If so, how long is it? _____

✤ How long is the news bulletin? _____

✤ Sort the programmes into categories such as sport, news, weather, drama, comedy, game shows.

✤ Which category is allocated the most time?
_____

Teacher Timesavers: Measurement skills

Name _____

Time

In a minute

In a minute

You will need: coloured pencils, a 1-minute timer, a ball.

✤ Work with a partner.

✤ Try each of these activities for 1 minute.

✤ Your partner will time you.

✤ Before you start, write your predictions in red pencil.

✤ Record your actual results in blue pencil.

✤ Make up another activity to complete in 1 minute.

✤ Record your results in the empty box.

I can bounce a ball ___ ___ times in 1 minute.

I can count to ___ ___ in 1 minute.

I can say the alphabet ___ ___ times in 1 minute.

I can run ___ ___ times round the field in 1 minute.

I can write my name ___ ___ times in 1 minute.

1 minute

Teacher Timesavers: Measurement skills

93

Time
Matching

Name _____

Matching

✤ Match each clock to the digital clock which shows the same time.

04:50

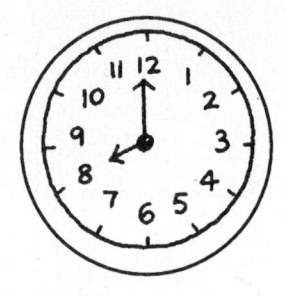

06:05

01:15

02:35

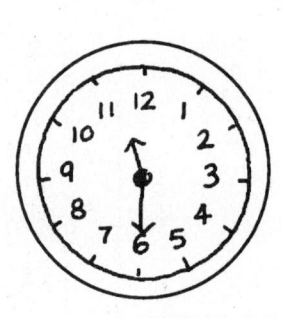

09:45

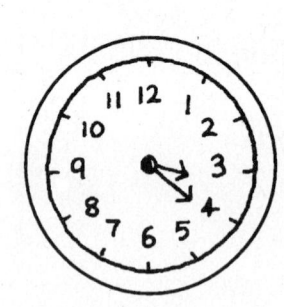

12:10

03:20

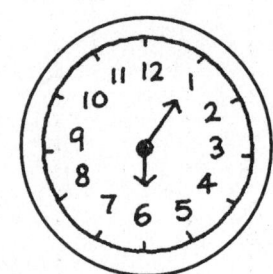

08:00

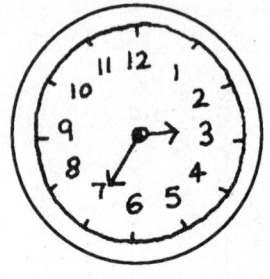

10:55

11:30

94

Teacher Timesavers: Measurement skills

Name _____

Time
Writing the date

Writing the date

There are two ways of writing dates:

- in full:
  5th May 1963
  29th March 1939

- using numbers only:
  05.05.63
  29.03.39

Each month can be represented by a number. **January** is **01**, **February 02** and so on.

✣ Complete this list of months:

January	**01**
February	**02**
March	
April	
May	
June	
July	
August	
September	
October	**10**
November	
December	

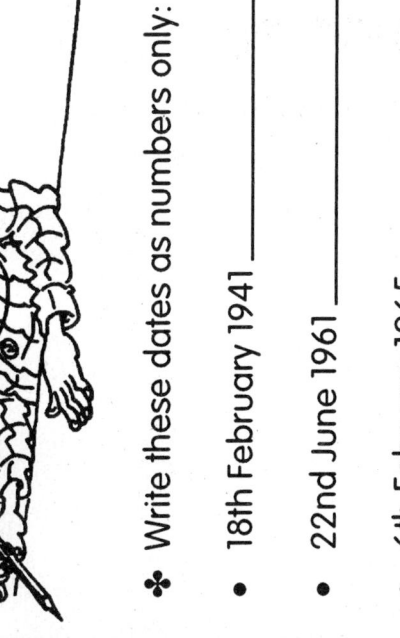

✣ Write these dates as numbers only:

- 18th February 1941 _____
- 22nd June 1961 _____
- 6th February 1965 _____
- 19th April 1969 _____

✣ Write these dates in full:

- 05.05.63 _____
- 07.11.81 _____
- 29.01.22 _____
- 16.12.90 _____

✣ Complete this table using the birthdates of your family members.

Name	Birthdate in full	Birthdate in numbers

Teacher Timesavers: Measurement skills

Time

Morning and afternoon

Name _____

Morning and afternoon

For times before noon we write **a.m.**
For times after noon we write **p.m.**

✤ Match each of the activities below with a suitable time.

- morning worship •   • 8.30 a.m.
- going to school •   • 5.45 a.m.
- watching an afternoon film •   • 10.30 a.m.
- going to bed •   • 8.45 a.m.
- going home from school •   • 2.15 p.m.
- sunrise •   • 8.30 p.m.
- the supermarket opens •   • 6.15 p.m.
- morning coffee •   • 10.45 a.m.
- sunset •   • 3.45 p.m.
- afternoon tea •   • 3.30 p.m.

✤ As the day passes, write down some of the things you do and the times. Remember to use **a.m.** or **p.m.**

At 3.00 p.m. it is the middle of the afternoon.

✤ Write a description of each of the following times:

- 7.00 a.m. _____

_____

- 11.30 p.m. _____

_____

- 10.15 a.m. _____

_____

- 1.30 a.m. _____

_____

Teacher Timesavers: Measurement skills

Name _____   Time
                                                                     Seconds

Seconds

You will need: a stopwatch, a pencil.

✤ Work with a partner.

✤ Use the stopwatch to time each activity.

✤ Before you start, write down your predictions.

✤ Then record your actual results.

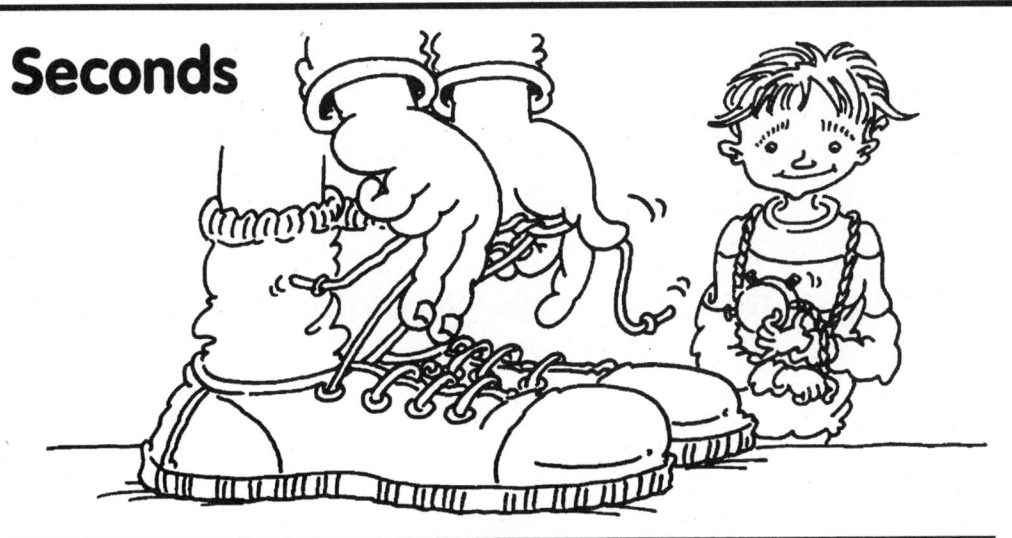

Name of activity	Prediction (seconds)	Time taken (seconds)
write my name five times		
tie my shoelace		
put on my jacket		
take off my shoes and socks		
say the alphabet		

✤ Think of some more activities to complete the table.

Teacher Timesavers: Measurement skills

Time
24-hour clocks

Name _____

24-hour clocks

Most clocks show only 12 hours, but there are 24 hours in each day/night. Sometimes we use **a.m.** or **p.m.** to distinguish between day times and night times. Another way of doing this is to use a 24-hour clock.

> 24-hour time is always written using four digits, for example:
> 2 p.m. is 14.00

♣ Use the 24-hour clock to write these times in 24-hour time:

- 3 p.m. _____
- 6 p.m. _____
- 8 a.m. _____
- Noon _____
- 10 p.m. _____

- Midnight _____
- 4 a.m. _____
- 9 p.m. _____
- 11 a.m. _____
- 7 p.m. _____

♣ Write these times using **a.m.** or **p.m.**

- 04.00 _____
- 08.00 _____
- 00.00 _____
- 12.00 _____
- 07.00 _____

- 18.00 _____
- 22.00 _____
- 01.00 _____
- 23.00 _____
- 16.00 _____

midnight 00
23 (11 p.m.)   12 noon   13 (1 p.m.)
11 a.m.   1 a.m.
22 (10 p.m.)   10 a.m.   2 a.m.   14 (2 p.m.)
21 (9 p.m.)   9 a.m.   3 a.m.   15 (3 p.m.)
8 a.m.   4 a.m.
20 (8 p.m.)   16 (4 p.m.)
7 a.m.   5 a.m.
19 (7 p.m.)   6 a.m.   17 (5 p.m.)
18 (6 p.m.)

♣ On the back of this sheet, make a list of the activities you do in one day. Use 24-hour time to show when you start and finish each activity.

Teacher Timesavers: Measurement skills

Tickets

The holders of these tickets do not know how to read 24-hour time.

♣ Explain what the 24-hour time on each one means.
Write your answers on the back of this sheet.
The first one is done for you.

FAST TRACK

From: Birmingham   10.30
To: Oxford   11.35
14.10.95   £14.95

The train leaves Birmingham at 10.30 in the morning and arrives 1 hour and 5 minutes later at 11.35.

TWO-WAY BUS COMPANY
GLASGOW 17.15
to PERTH 20.22

15.10.95

CINEMA 1
ADMIT 1   20:15

McREEVIE CASTLE
ADMIT 1
Last Admission 17.15
16.10.95

BAIRD'S GARDEN PARTY
11.00 –16.30
Lunch will be served
12.30 –13.30
Cost £2.50

ALL-DAY
ROCK CONCERT
GATES OPEN **09.00**
GATES CLOSE **00.00**

TASQA AIRWAYS LTD

COOK MR C				
FROM	CARRIER	FLIGHT	DATE	TIME
PERTH	TQ	448	15 JUL	0600
TO SINGAPORE	TQ	501	16 JUL	1700
TO LONDON	VOID			

Teacher Timesavers: Measurement skills

Time
Triathlon times

Name _____

Triathlon times

The table below gives the starting and finishing times for each stage of a triathlon.

✤ Use this information to work out the total time it took for each competitor to complete the triathlon.
It is easiest to work in minutes.

Name	Swim			Cycle			Run			Total time taken (minutes)
	Start	Finish	Time	Start	Finish	Time	Start	Finish	Time	
Ayman	10.00	10.47		13.00	14.58		15.30	16.15		
Gary	10.00	11.03		13.00	14.37		15.30	16.32		
Nicole	10.00	11.14		13.00	14.05		15.30	16.30		
Anthony	10.00	11.00		13.00	14.17		15.30	16.08		
Dan	10.00	10.42		13.00	15.01		15.30	16.25		
Silla	10.00	10.41		13.00	14.19		15.30	16.09		

✤ Complete the roll of honour.   1st _____   2nd _____   3rd _____   4th _____

Teacher Timesavers: Measurement skills

Name _____

Time

Babysitting

Babysitting

This table shows the times Janine has babysat during November.

November

Name	Date	Start time	Finish time	Total time Rounded up	Money earned
Hunter	06.11.95	18.00	21.30		
Stephens	08.11.95	17.30	22.45		
MacLeod	10.11.95	09.45	12.37		
Jones	10.11.95	20.15	00.15		
Hunter	15.11.95	09.00	15.21		
Hunter	16.11.95	09.00	20.18		
MacLeod	21.11.95	16.40	17.54		
Jones	27.11.95	17.15	23.17		
Jones	28.11.95	17.15	23.55		
Hunter	30.11.95	08.30	14.36		
				Total earnings	

♣ Complete the table by working out how long each job took and how much Janine earned.

She charges £2.50 per hour plus 50p for each extra quarter hour.

All times are rounded up to the nearest quarter hour. For example, if she worked 2 hours 17 minutes she would charge for 2 hours 30 minutes.

♣ How much did each family pay?

• Hunter _____ • Stephens _____

• MacLeod _____ • Jones _____

♣ Which family is her best client?

_____

Why? _____

Teacher Timesavers: Measurement skills

Time

Speed

Name _____

Speed

You will need: a trundle wheel, a stopwatch, a calculator, a pencil.

✣ Use a trundle wheel to measure out a distance of 200m.

✣ Time at least ten of your classmates running over this distance.

✣ Record your results in the table below.

✣ Use a calculator to work out each person's speed.

Name	Distance (metres)	Time taken (seconds)	Speed(m/s) = $\frac{distance}{time}$

✣ Now answer these questions.

• Who travelled at the highest speed?

_____

• Who travelled at the lowest speed?

_____

• Calculate the average speed of the group.

• How does your own speed compare with the average?

_____

Teacher Timesavers: Measurement skills

Name _____

Perimeter

How far round?

How far round?

You will need: a red pencil.

For each pair:

✤ Trace the perimeter of each thing with a red pencil.

✤ Draw a cross on the one with the greater 'distance around'.

football pitch	netball court

stamp	envelope

this page	classroom

hopscotch	chessboard

Teacher Timesavers: Measurement skills

Perimeter

Measuring perimeters

Name _____

Measuring perimeters

You will need: a ruler, a trundle wheel, a tape measure, a metre ruler, a pencil.

✤ Measure the perimeter of each of the objects listed in the table.

✤ Before you start, predict what the measurement will be.

✤ List the measuring devices you used.

✤ Complete the table by measuring some more objects.

Object	Measuring device	Estimate of perimeter	Perimeter
this page			
the chalkboard			
a desktop/tabletop			
a hoop			

Name _____

Perimeter

Solve the riddle

♣ Calculate the perimeter of each shape.

♣ Match each answer to a letter to solve the riddle.

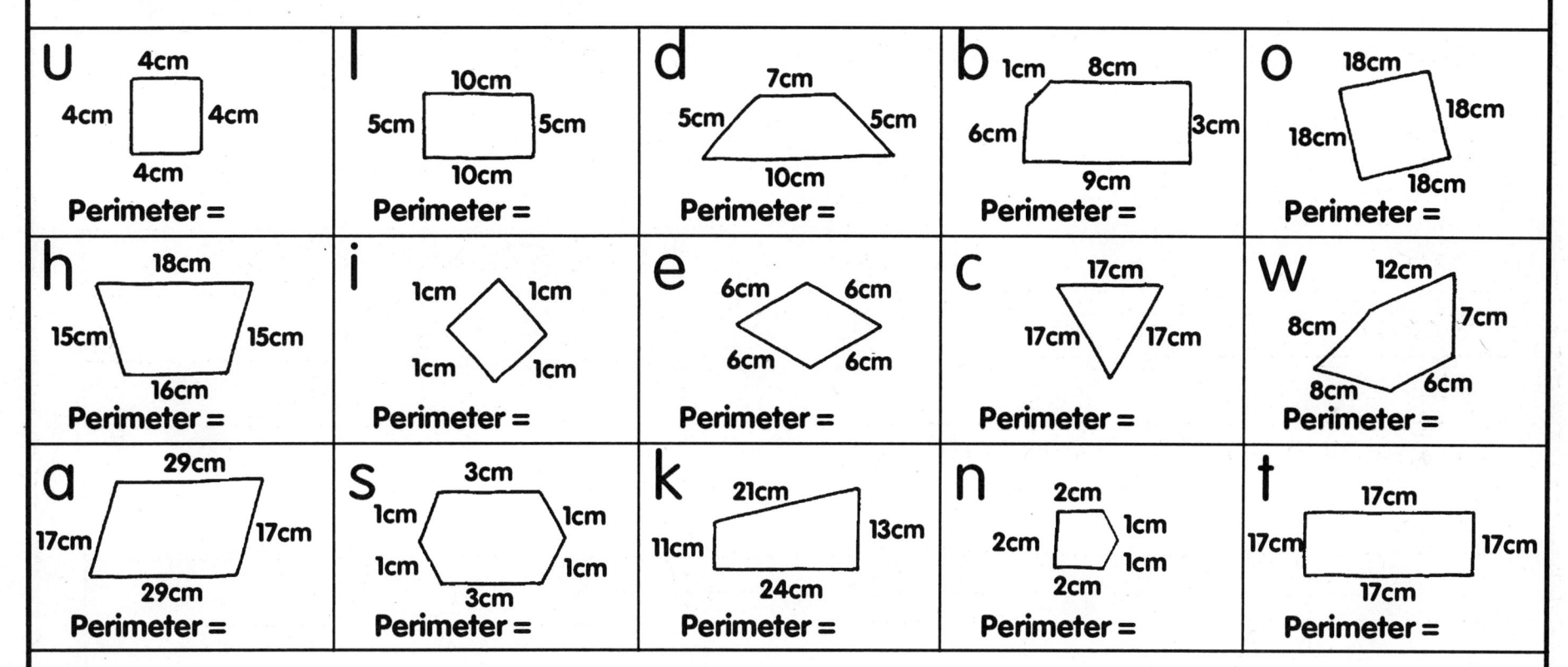

u 4cm square (4cm, 4cm, 4cm) Perimeter =	**l** rectangle 10cm × 5cm Perimeter =	**d** trapezoid 7cm top, 5cm sides, 10cm bottom Perimeter =	**b** pentagon 1cm, 8cm, 3cm, 9cm, 6cm Perimeter =	**o** rhombus 18cm all sides Perimeter =
h trapezoid 18cm top, 15cm sides, 16cm bottom Perimeter =	**i** rhombus 1cm all sides Perimeter =	**e** rhombus 6cm all sides Perimeter =	**c** triangle 17cm all sides Perimeter =	**w** quadrilateral 12cm, 7cm, 6cm, 8cm, 8cm Perimeter =
a parallelogram 29cm, 17cm Perimeter =	**s** hexagon 3cm, 1cm, 1cm, 3cm, 1cm, 1cm Perimeter =	**k** trapezoid 21cm, 13cm, 24cm, 11cm Perimeter =	**n** pentagon 2cm, 1cm, 1cm, 2cm, 2cm Perimeter =	**t** rectangle 17cm × 17cm Perimeter =

What makes the letter **t** so important to a stick insect?

41 4 56 64 72 16 56   4 56,   4 56   41 72 16 30 27   32 24   92   10 4 51 69   4 8 10 24 51 56

Teacher Timesavers: Measurement skills

105

Perimeter

Borders

Name _____

Borders

You will need: a metre ruler, a pencil.

♣ Measure the perimeter of each of the display boards in your classroom.

♣ Record your work like this:

```
                3m 20cm
                3m 20cm
                1m 50cm
            +   1m 50cm
Perimeter   =   9m 40 cm
```

3m 20cm

1m 50cm

♣ If you were going to put new borders round all the display boards, how much border material would be required altogether?

_____

♣ If border material costs £1.25 per metre, how much would it cost?

_____

Name _____

Perimeter

Squares

Squares

You will need: a pencil, a centimetre ruler.

♣ Find the perimeter of each of these squares by adding the lengths of the sides. The first one is done for you.

1cm ☐

Perimeter =
  1cm
  1cm
  1cm
+ 1cm
  ———
  4cm

Perimeter =

Perimeter =

Perimeter =

Perimeter =

♣ Is there an easy way to find the perimeter of a square?

Explain your idea. _____

_____

_____

♣ Use your idea to calculate the perimeter of an 18cm square.

Teacher Timesavers: Measurement skills

Perimeter

Rectangles

Name _____

Rectangles

You will need: a pencil, a centimetre ruler.

♣ Find the perimeter of each of these rectangles by adding the lengths of the sides. The first one is done for you.

```
       3cm
   ┌─────────┐
2cm│         │2cm
   └─────────┘
       3cm
```

Perimeter =
  3cm
  2cm
  3cm
+ 2cm
─────
 10cm

Perimeter =

Perimeter =

Perimeter =

Perimeter =

♣ Is there an easy way to find the perimeter of a rectangle?

Explain your idea. _____

_____

_____

108

Teacher Timesavers: Measurement skills

Name _____

Perimeter

Christmas lights

Christmas lights

Each of the shapes **A–D** is going to be decorated with Christmas lights. The lights will be attached to the outside of the shape, like this:

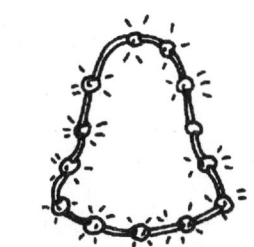

✤ Calculate how many metres of lighting are required for each shape, and how many metres are required altogether.

A 2m × 2m

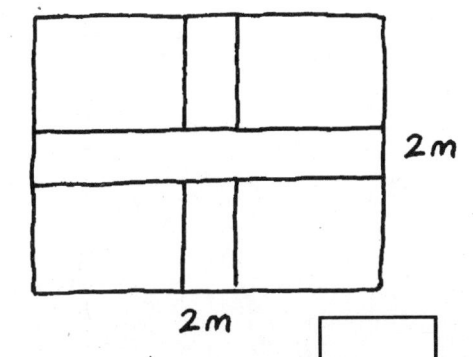

☐ m

B 1m, 1.5m

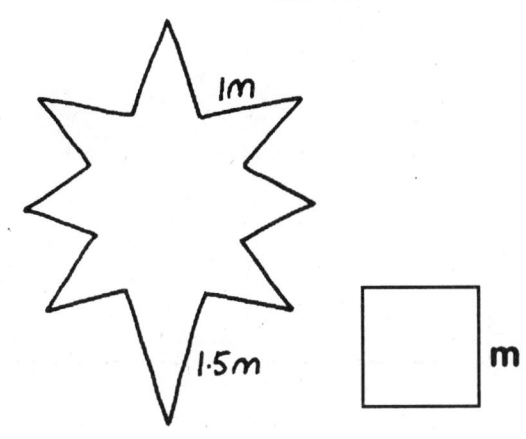

☐ m

C 3.5m, 1m

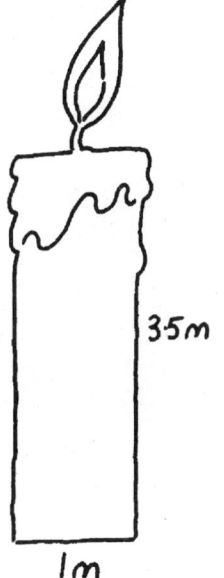

☐ m

D 0.5m, 20cm, 1m, 40cm, 2m, 80cm, 30cm, 30cm

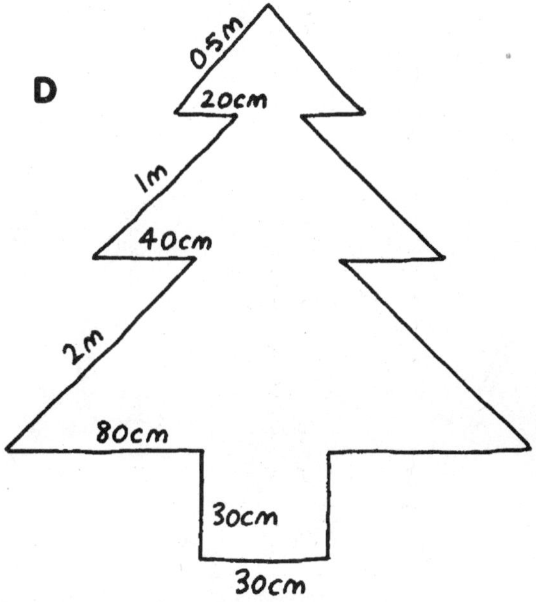

☐ m

☐ m are required altogether.

Teacher Timesavers: Measurement skills   109

Perimeter

Swimming pools

Name _____

Swimming pools

A fence is going to be built round each of these swimming pools.
The fencing costs £22.50 per metre.

✤ Work out the amount of fencing required for each pool, and the cost involved.

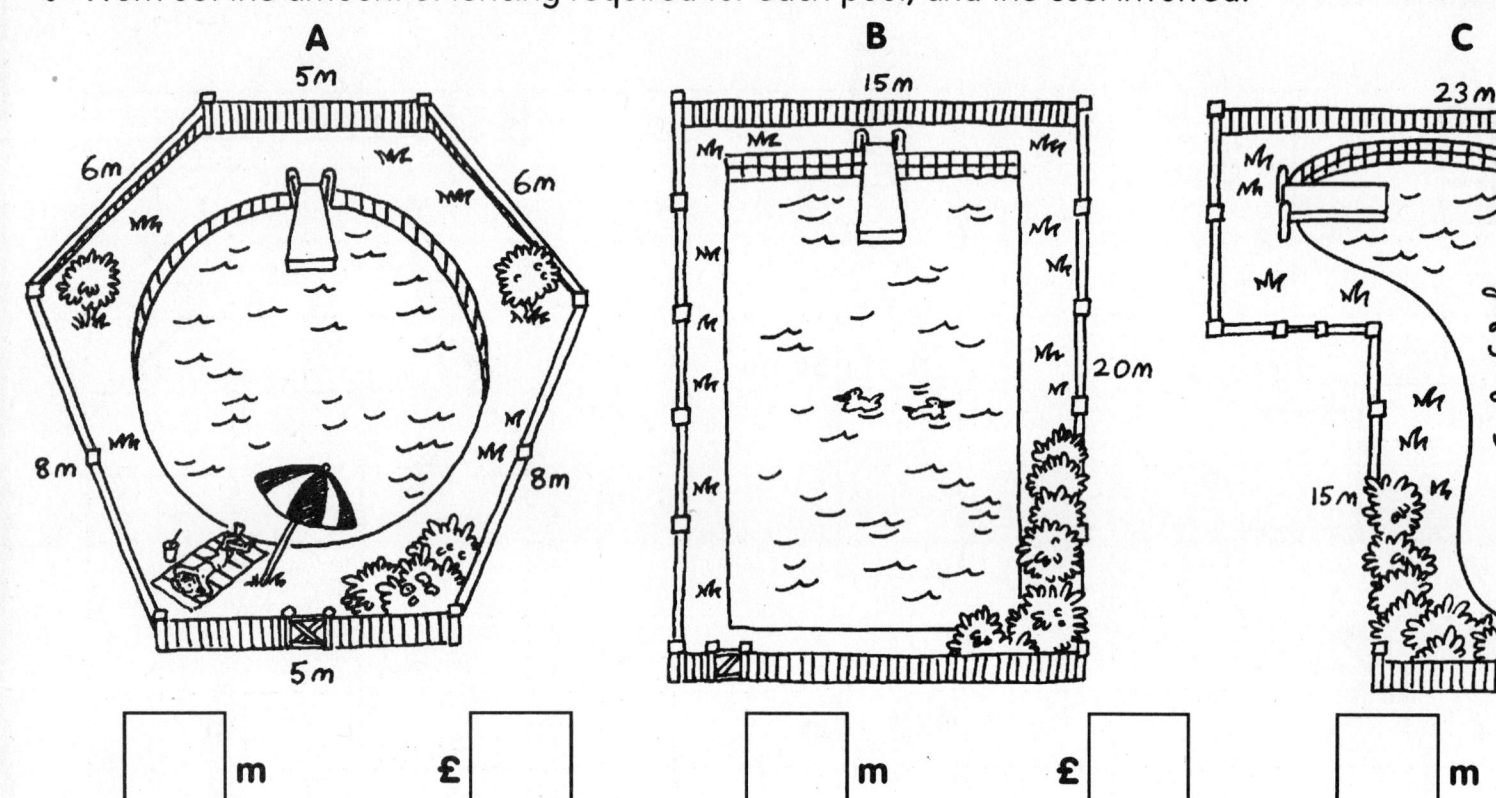

A
- 5m (top)
- 6m, 6m
- 8m, 8m
- 5m (bottom)

B
- 15m
- 20m

C
- 23m (top)
- 23m (right)
- 15m (bottom right)
- 15m (bottom left)

☐ m ☐ £   ☐ m ☐ £   ☐ m ☐ £

✤ Which pool will be the cheapest to fence? ☐   ✤ Which will be the most expensive? ☐

110   Teacher Timesavers: Measurement skills

Name _____

Perimeter

Squared paper

You will need: a pencil, a centimetre ruler.

♣ Draw as many different shapes as you can that have a perimeter of 16cm. Each square measures 1cm × 1cm.

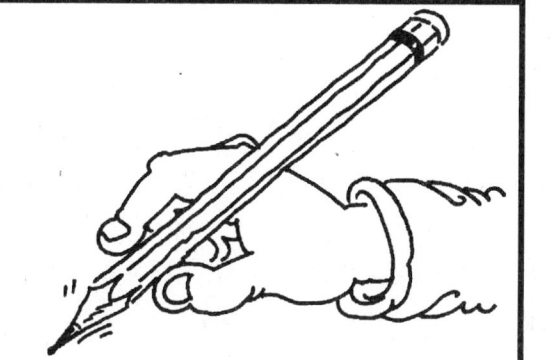

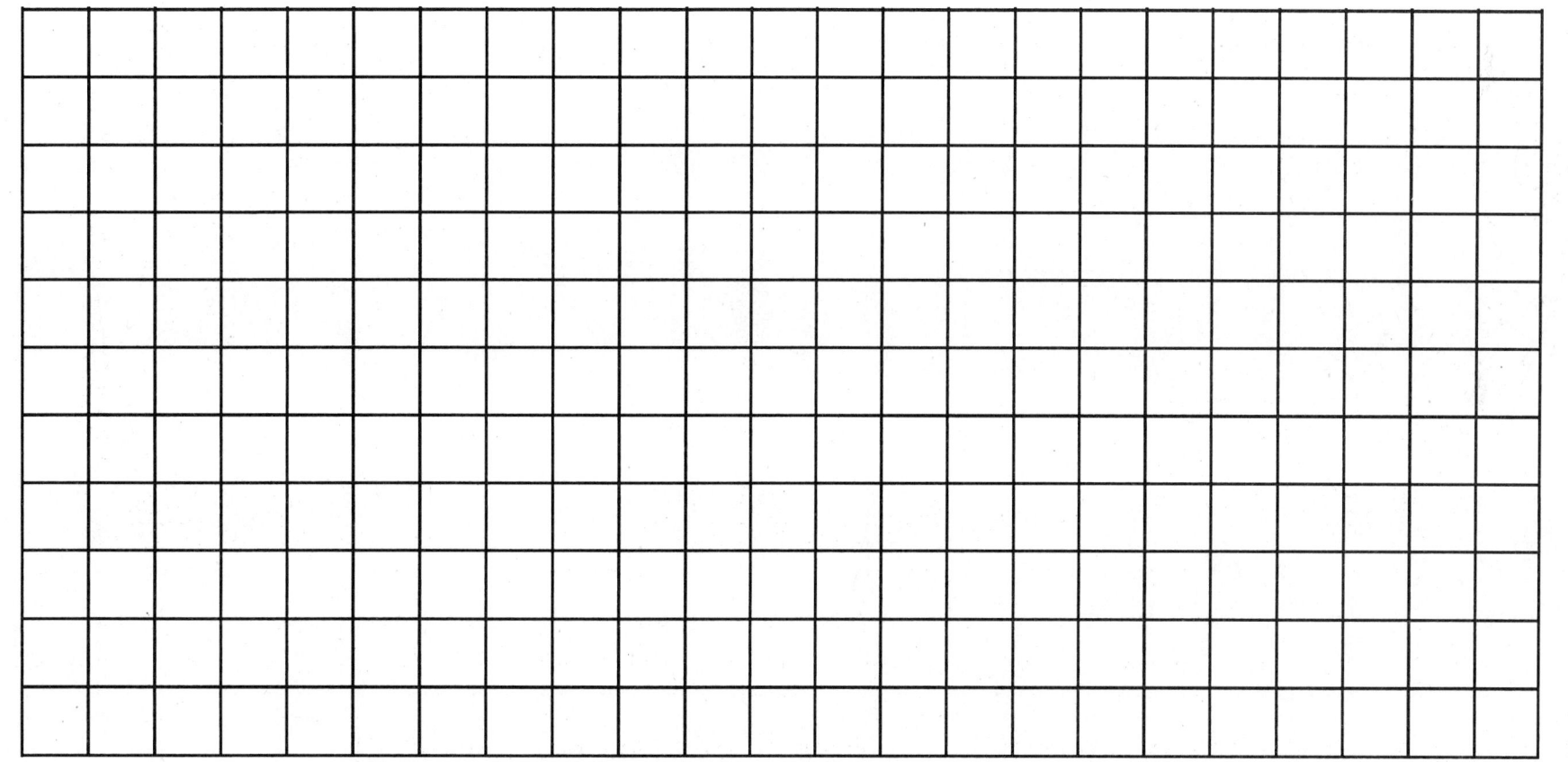

Teacher Timesavers: Measurement skills

Perimeter

Regular polygons

Name _____

Regular polygons

Regular polygons have all sides equal in length.

You will need: a pencil, a centimetre ruler.

♣ Measure the sides of each polygon.

♣ Calculate the perimeter of each polygon.

octagon

Perimeter =

square

Perimeter =

hexagon

Perimeter =

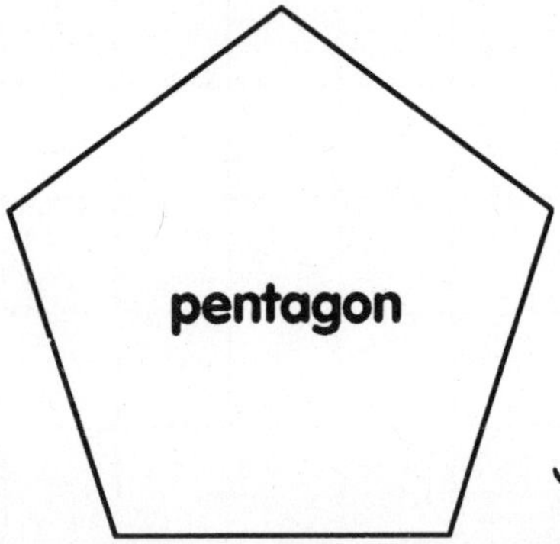

pentagon

Perimeter =

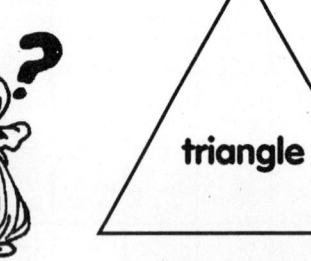

triangle

Perimeter =

heptagon

Perimeter =

♣ Explain how you found the perimeters. Did you use multiplication or addition?

_____

_____

112   Teacher Timesavers: Measurement skills

Name _____

Perimeter

Different shapes

Different shapes

You will need: a pencil, a centimetre ruler.

The shape on the right has a perimeter of 24cm.

✤ In the space below, draw as many different shapes as you can which have a perimeter of 24cm.

Teacher Timesavers: Measurement skills

Perimeter
On the farm

Name _____

On the farm

You will need: a pencil, a calculator.

This is a plan of Farmer Donald's fields.
He has recently been given a grant from the EU to replace all his fences.

♣ Calculate the total amount of fencing required. _____

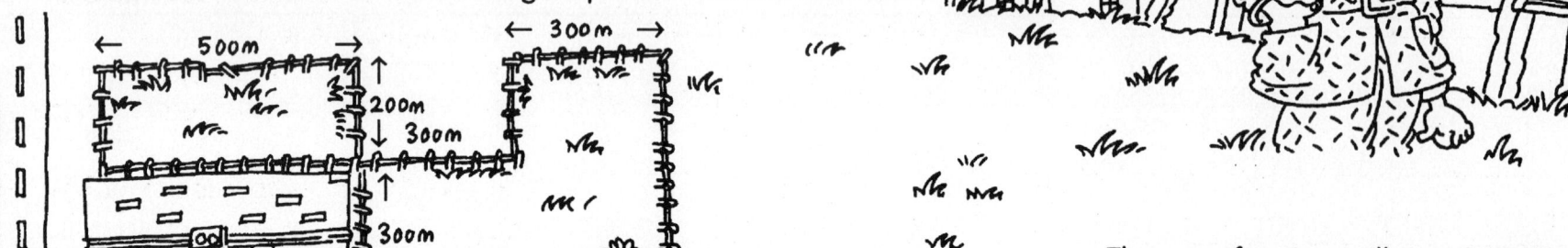

The new fencing will cost £18.50 per metre.

♣ How much will Farmer Donald's fencing cost?

_____

The EU will pay 55% of the cost.

♣ How much will Farmer Donald have to pay?

_____

Teacher Timesavers: Measurement skills

Name _____

Perimeter
Doubling up

Doubling up

You will need: a pencil, a centimetre ruler.

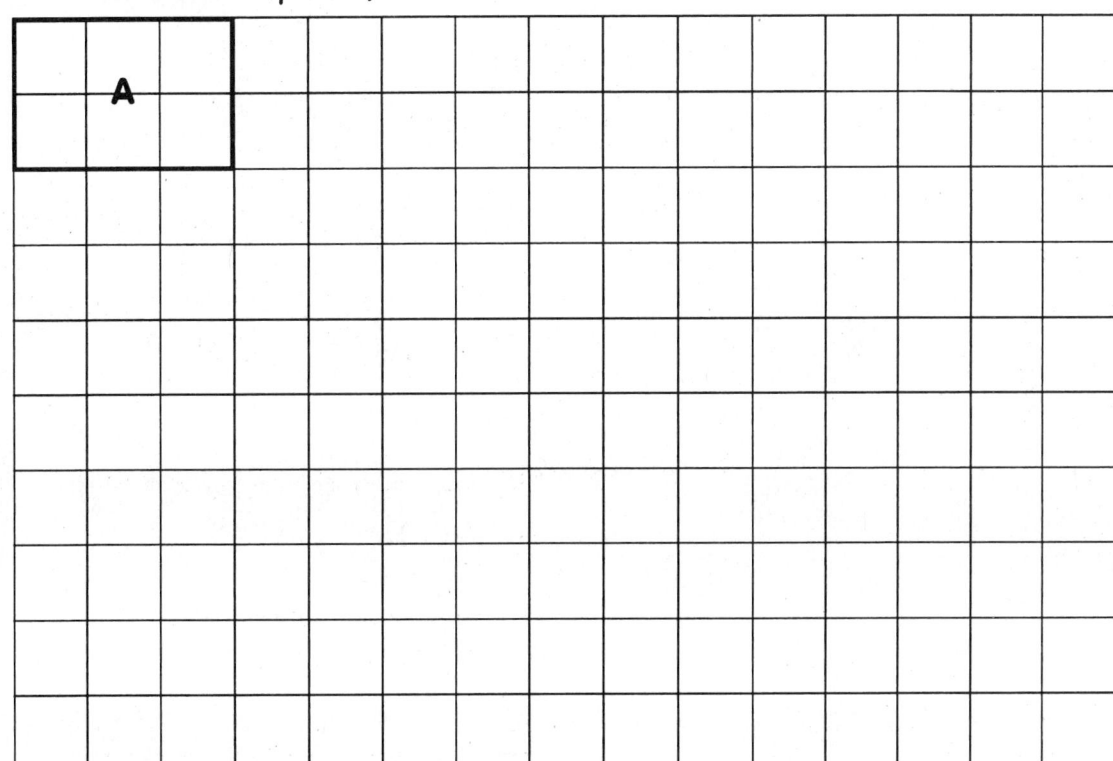

✤ Double and triple the lengths of the sides of rectangle **A** to make rectangles **B** and **C**.

✤ Calculate the perimeter of each rectangle.
Each square measures 1cm × 1cm.

Rectangle	Perimeter
A	
B	
C	
D	

✤ Study the results carefully.
Can you see a pattern? Explain._____
_____

✤ Predict the perimeter of rectangle **D** (with sides four times longer than those of rectangle **A**).

✤ Draw this shape and check your prediction.

Teacher Timesavers: Measurement skills

Perimeter

Lakes

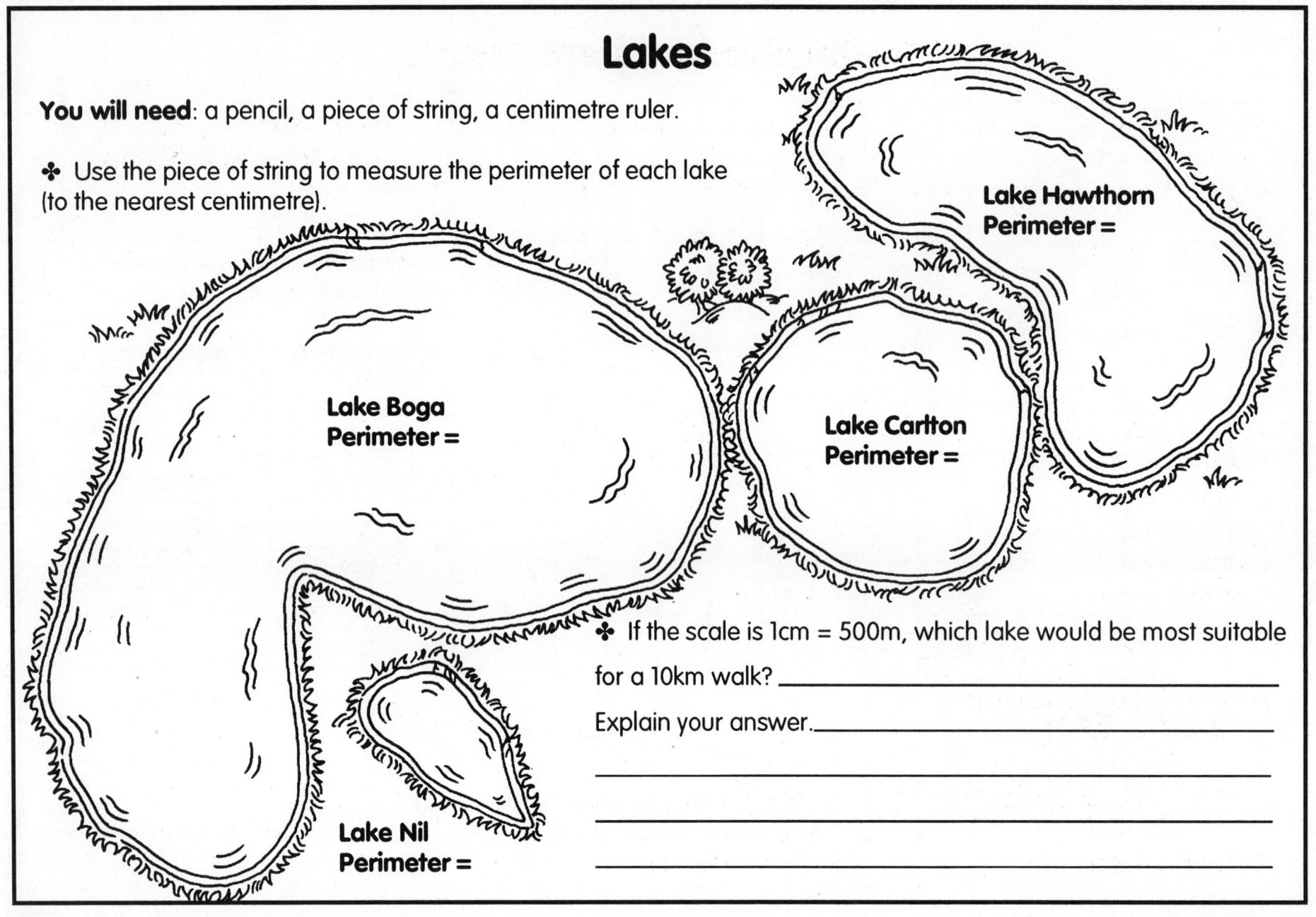

Name _____

You will need: a pencil, a piece of string, a centimetre ruler.

♣ Use the piece of string to measure the perimeter of each lake (to the nearest centimetre).

Lake Hawthorn Perimeter =

Lake Boga Perimeter =

Lake Carlton Perimeter =

Lake Nil Perimeter =

♣ If the scale is 1cm = 500m, which lake would be most suitable for a 10km walk? _____

Explain your answer. _____

_____

_____

_____

Name _____

Perimeter

Perimeter problems

Perimeter problems (cards)

Cut

The playground of a school is rectangular. Its length is 125m and its width is 63m. Tony walks all the way round it twice.

♣ How far has he walked?

Draw a square which has a perimeter of 16cm.

A field is 8km long and 4km wide. It is fenced with three rows of wire.

♣ How much wire is needed to fence the field?

Joan's garden is square and has an area of 36m².

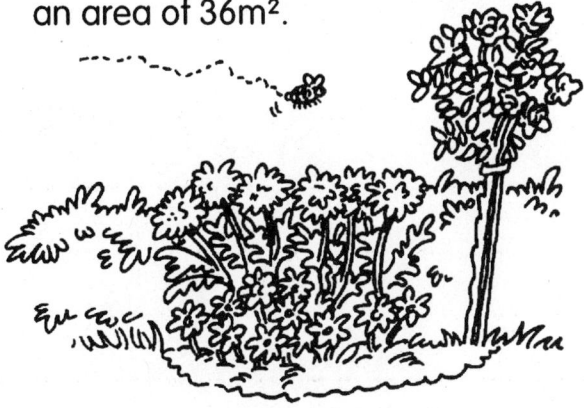

♣ What is its perimeter?

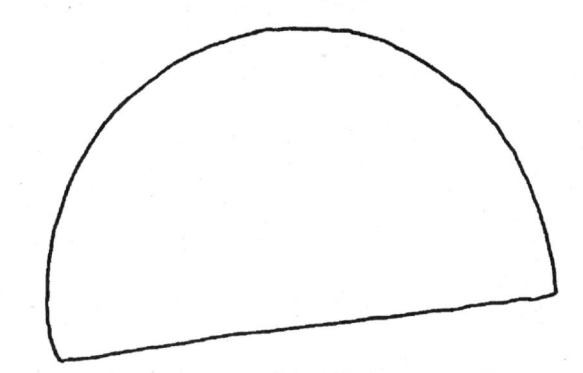

♣ Discuss how you would measure the perimeter of this shape.
♣ Try out your ideas.

Hu-Chen wants to build a brick border round his tulip garden.

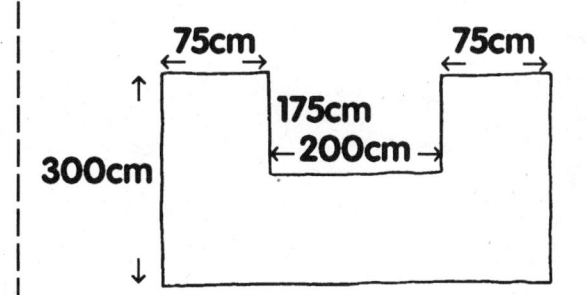

75cm   75cm
175cm
←200cm→
300cm

♣ If each brick is 35cm long, how many will he need?

Teacher Timesavers: Measurement skills

117

Perimeter

Find the perimeter

Name _____

Find the perimeter

✤ Find the perimeter of each of these shapes.
You may need to convert some of the measurements to a different unit before adding.

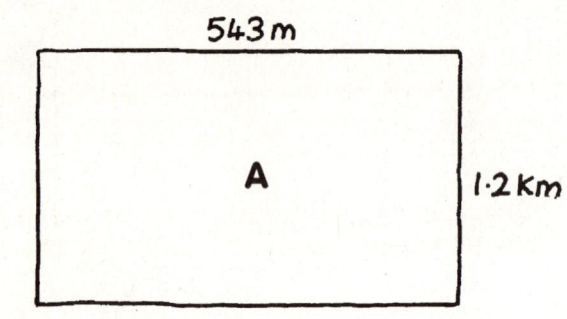

A: 543 m, 1.2 km

Perimeter =

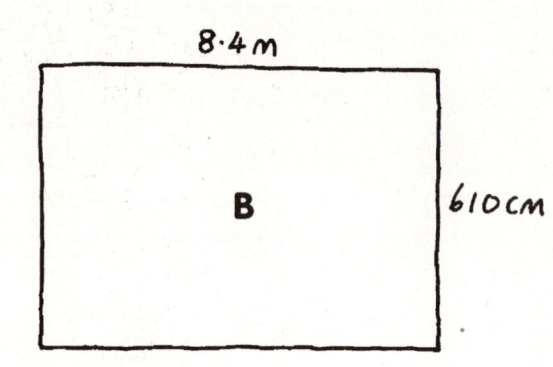

B: 8.4 m, 610 cm

Perimeter =

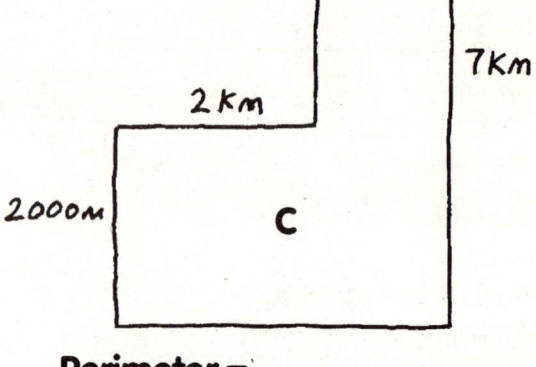

C: 1 km, 7 km, 2 km, 2000 m

Perimeter =

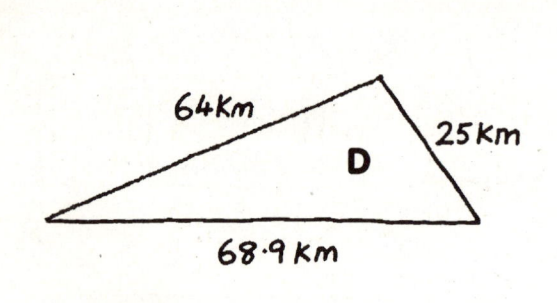

D: 64 km, 25 km, 68.9 km

Perimeter =

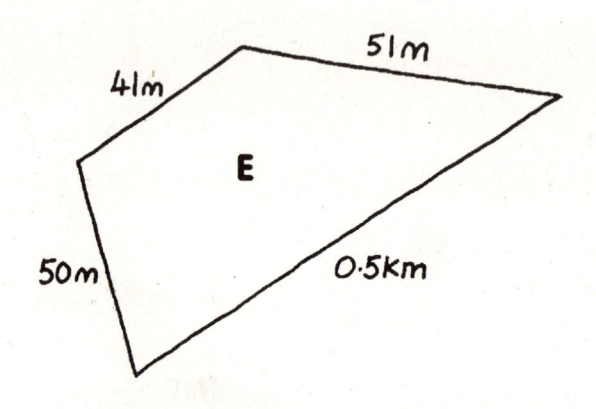

E: 41 m, 51 m, 50 m, 0.5 km

Perimeter =

F: 518 m, 514 m, 511 m, 516 m, 525 m, 0.75 km

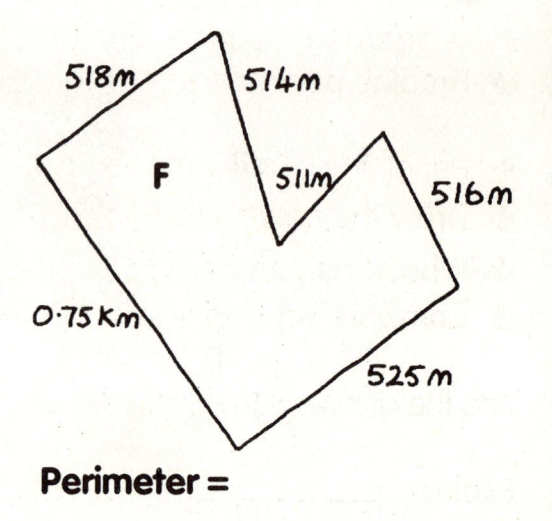

Perimeter =

Name _____

Perimeter

Joining shapes

Joining shapes

You will need: a centimetre ruler, a pencil, paper, scissors.

Find the perimeter of each shape.

A _____   B _____

C _____   D _____

✤ Which two shapes have the same perimeter? _____

✤ Cut out the shapes.
✤ Put the following shapes together.

A + B _____   A + C _____   A + D _____

✤ Find the perimeters of the new shapes.

✤ Put all the shapes together.
✤ Draw the new shape on another piece of paper.
✤ What is its perimeter? _____
✤ Compare your answer with those of some friends.

Are the answers the same? _____

Explain. _____

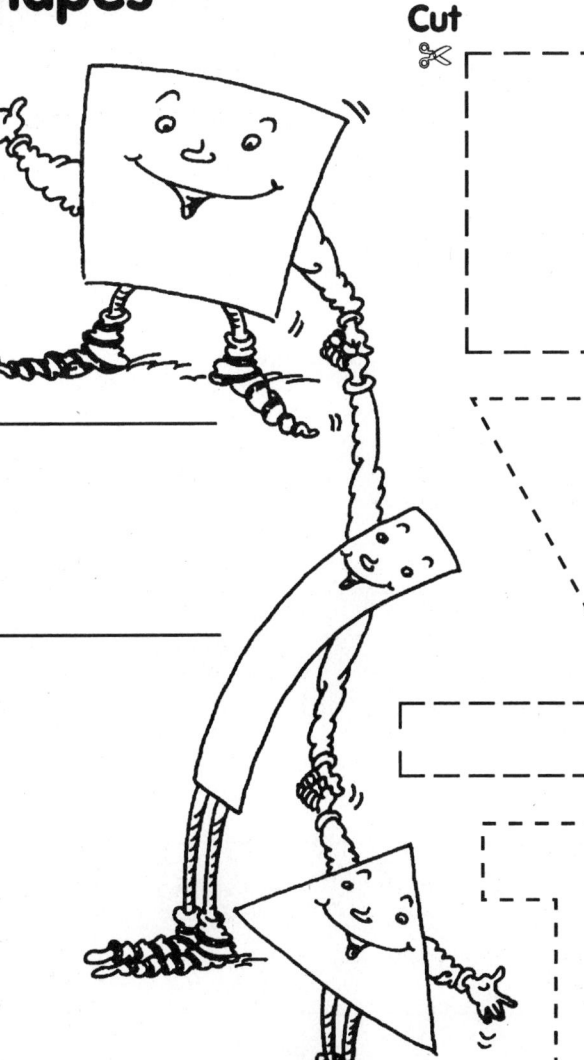

Cut

A

B

C

D

Teacher Timesavers: Measurement skills

Perimeter

Athletics

Name _____

Athletics

This is a plan of a running track.

120m

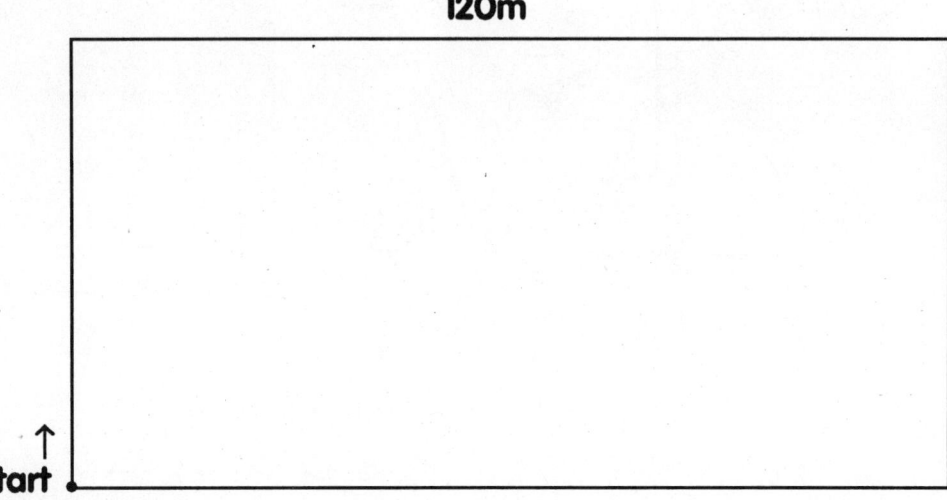

60m

↑
Start

✤ For each of these races, describe how many times the runners will have to go round the track.

- 100 metres _____
- 120-metre hurdles _____
- 200 metres _____
- 400 metres _____

- 800 metres _____
- 1000 metres _____
- 5 kilometres _____
- 10 kilometres _____

Teacher Timesavers: Measurement skills

Name _____

Perimeter

Warm-up

These are the courts used for four different ball games.
Each player warms up by jogging round the court three times.

♣ Calculate how far each player runs.

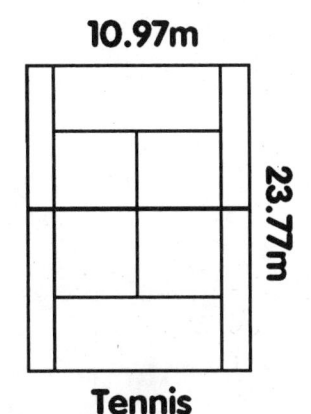

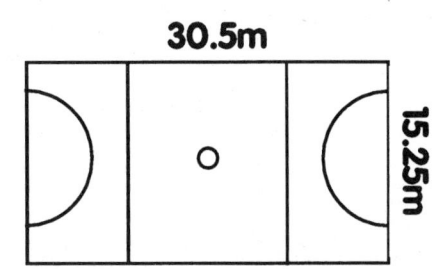

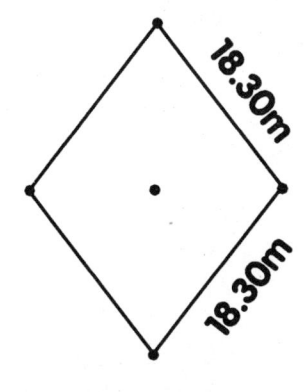

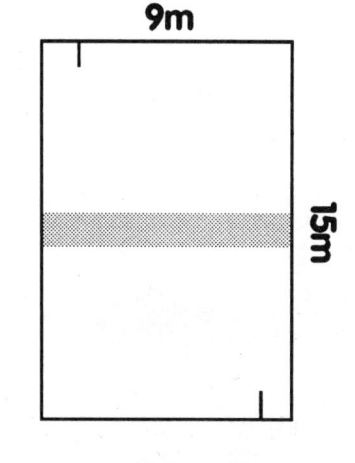

Tennis — 10.97m × 23.77m

Netball — 30.5m × 15.25m

Baseball — 18.30m (rhombus, all sides 18.30m)

Volleyball — 9m × 15m

_____   _____   _____   _____

♣ Who runs the furthest? _____   Who runs the least distance? _____

The new fitness coach recommends that each player runs five times round the court as a warm-up.

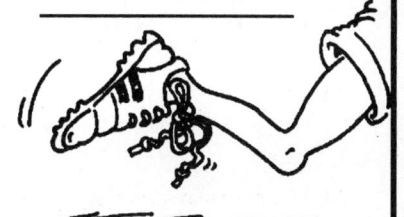

♣ Calculate the distance they will each have to run now. _____ _____ _____ _____

♣ Do any of them run further than 1km? _____

Teacher Timesavers: Measurement skills

121

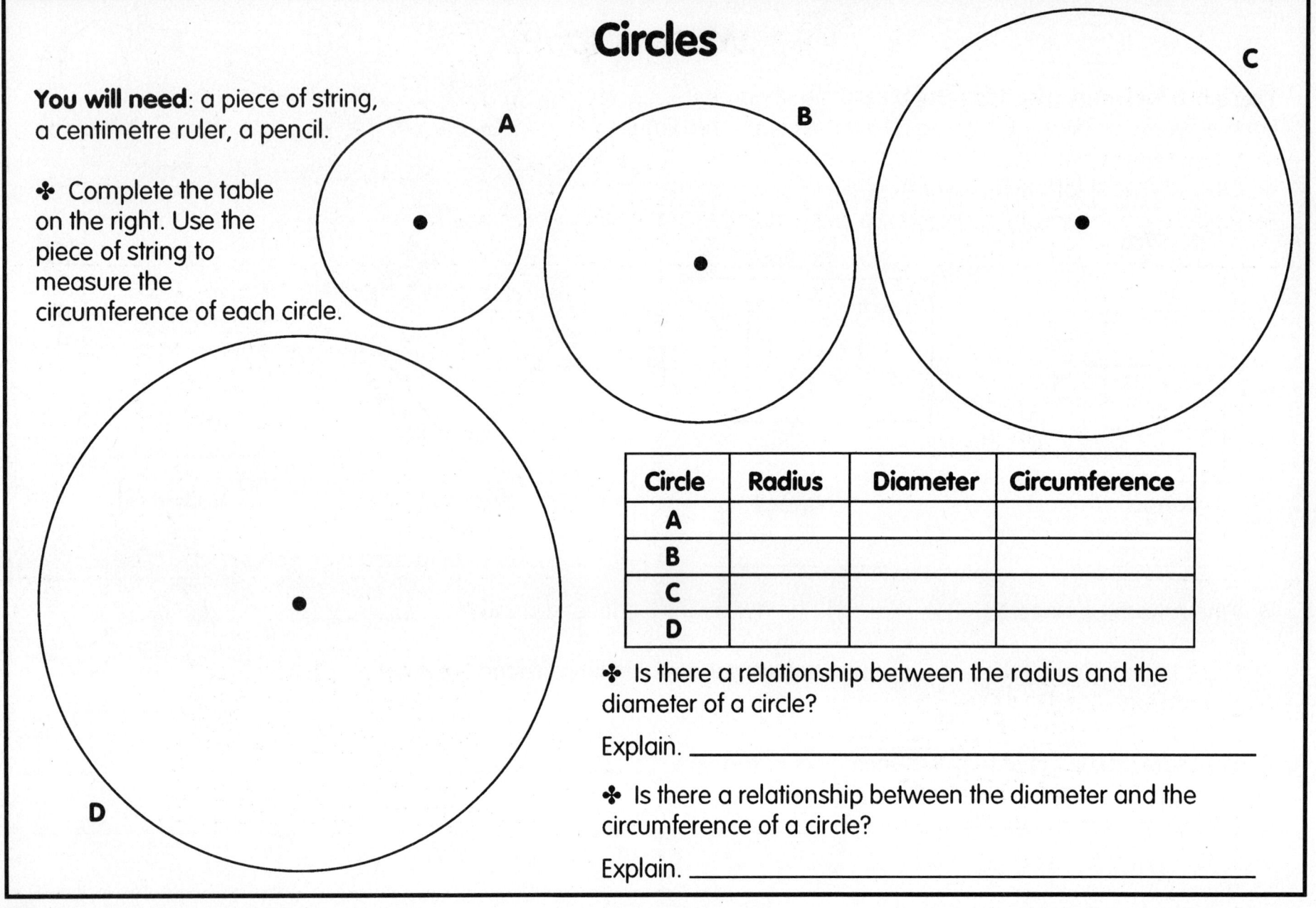

Perimeter

Circles

Name _____

Circles

You will need: a piece of string, a centimetre ruler, a pencil.

♣ Complete the table on the right. Use the piece of string to measure the circumference of each circle.

Circle	Radius	Diameter	Circumference
A			
B			
C			
D			

♣ Is there a relationship between the radius and the diameter of a circle?

Explain. _____

♣ Is there a relationship between the diameter and the circumference of a circle?

Explain. _____

Teacher Timesavers: Measurement skills

Name _____   *Area*

Large and small

You will need: scissors, paste, paper.

✤ Cut out these pictures.

✤ Paste them in order on a sheet of paper, starting with the thing which has the largest area.

Cut

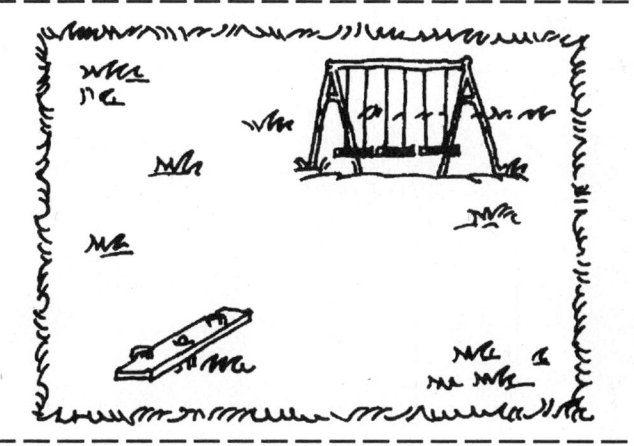

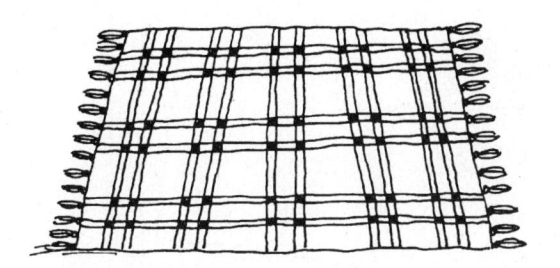

Teacher Timesavers: Measurement skills   123

Area

Larger or smaller?

You will need: coloured pencils.

♣ On the back of this sheet, make a list of objects that cover a larger area than this page.

♣ Now make a list of objects that cover a smaller area than this page.

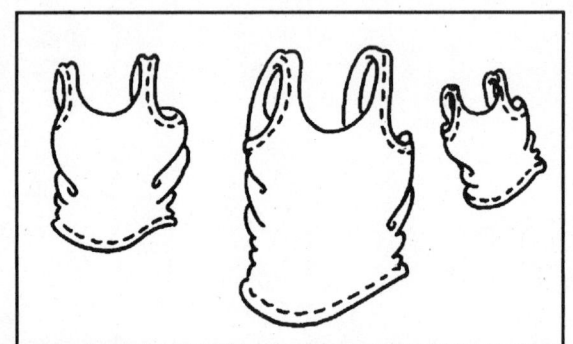

♣ Colour the one with the largest area:

♣ Colour the one with the smallest area:

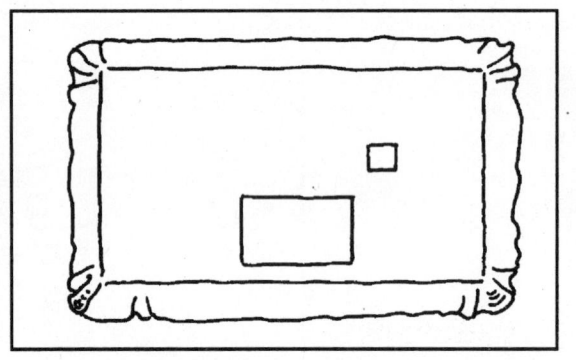

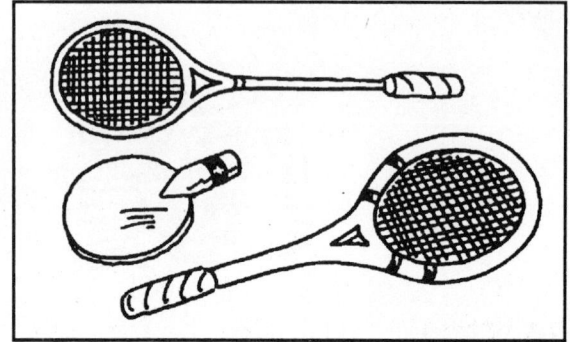

Name _____

Area

Measuring with blocks

Measuring with blocks

You will need: six small flat objects, a pencil, interlocking cubes such as Multilink or Unifix.

♣ Guess how many blocks it will take to cover each object.

♣ Write your predictions below.

♣ Use blocks to measure the area of each object.

♣ Draw the objects and write your answers below.

Prediction: about 4 blocks
Area: 2 × 2 blocks

Prediction:
Area:

Prediction:
Area:

Prediction:
Area:

Prediction:
Area:

Prediction:
Area:

Teacher Timesavers: Measurement skills

Area
Measuring with books

Name _____

Measuring with books

You will need: a pencil, a set of books which are all the same size.

♣ Guess how many books you will need to cover each of the surfaces listed in the table.

♣ Cover each of the surfaces with books.

♣ Write your predictions and results in the table.

♣ List the surfaces in order, starting with the one with the smallest area.

♣ Choose some more surfaces to measure and complete the table.

Surface	Prediction (books)	Area (books)
my desk/table top		
the teacher's desk top		
a page of a newspaper		
the top of a bookshelf		

_____
_____
_____
_____
_____
_____
_____
_____
_____
_____
_____

Teacher Timesavers: Measurement skills

Name _____

Area

Measuring with newspaper

Measuring with newspaper

You will need: a pencil, some newspapers which are all the same size.

❖ Guess how many newspaper pages you will need to cover each of the surfaces listed in the table.

❖ Cover each of the surfaces with newspaper pages.

❖ Write your predictions and results in the table.

Surface	Prediction (newspaper pages)	Area (newspaper pages)
the teacher's desk top		
the classroom floor		
the corridor floor		
the cloakroom floor		
my desk/table top		

❖ Complete the table below by matching each surface to the most appropriate measuring unit. Write the name of the object in the correct box.

Objects
- a postcard
- a ruler
- the classroom floor
- a poster
- a stamp
- a doormat
- the playground
- a coin
- my desk/table top
- a book
- this page
- a window

Blocks	Books	Newspaper

Teacher Timesavers: Measurement skills

127

Area
Geoboards

Name _____

Geoboards

You will need: a geoboard, rubber bands, a pencil.

♣ Use the geoboard and rubber bands to create three shapes, each with an area of six square units.

♣ Record your work on the grids below.

Name _____

Area

Alphabet area

Alphabet area

You will need: coloured pencils, a centimetre ruler, centimetre-squared paper.

✤ Find the area of each of the letters below.

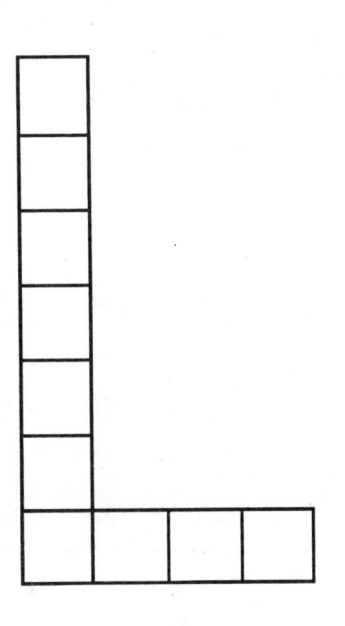

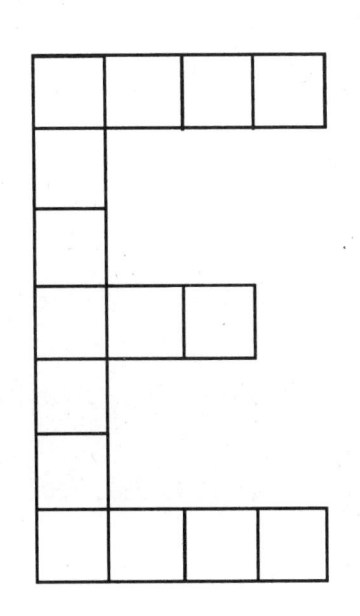

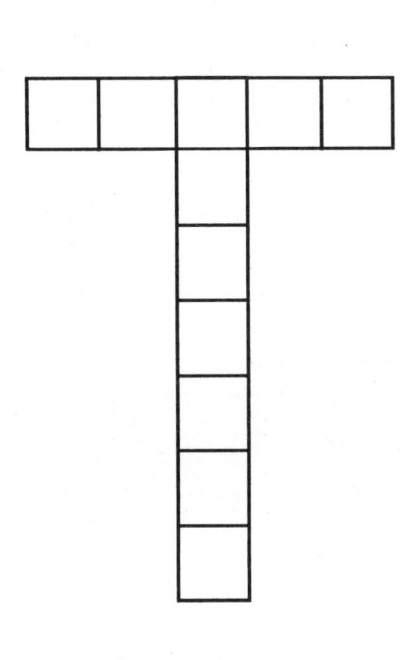

Area =

Area =

Area =

✤ On centimetre-squared paper, draw and colour the letters of your first name (in capitals).

✤ Calculate the area of each letter and then the total area of your name.

Area
Hands

Hands

You will need: centimetre-squared paper, a pencil.

♣ Trace your hand on a sheet of centimetre-squared paper.

♣ Count the squares and parts of squares to find the approximate area of your hand.

♣ Record your results and those of some of your classmates in the table below.

Name	Area of hand (squares)	Height (cm)

♣ Now measure your height, and record your results and those of your classmates in the table.

♣ Who is the tallest person? _____
Who has the largest hands? _____
Are they the same person? _____

♣ Who is the shortest person? _____
Who has the smallest hands? _____
Are they the same person? _____

♣ List your classmates in order on the back of this sheet, starting with the person with the smallest hands.

♣ Now list your classmates in order, starting with the shortest person.

♣ What do you notice? _____

Teacher Timesavers: Measurement skills

Name _____

Area

Leaves

Leaves

You will need: a collection of different leaves, a pencil.

✤ Choose four of the leaves, and draw round them on the grid below.

✤ Label the leaves **A–D**.

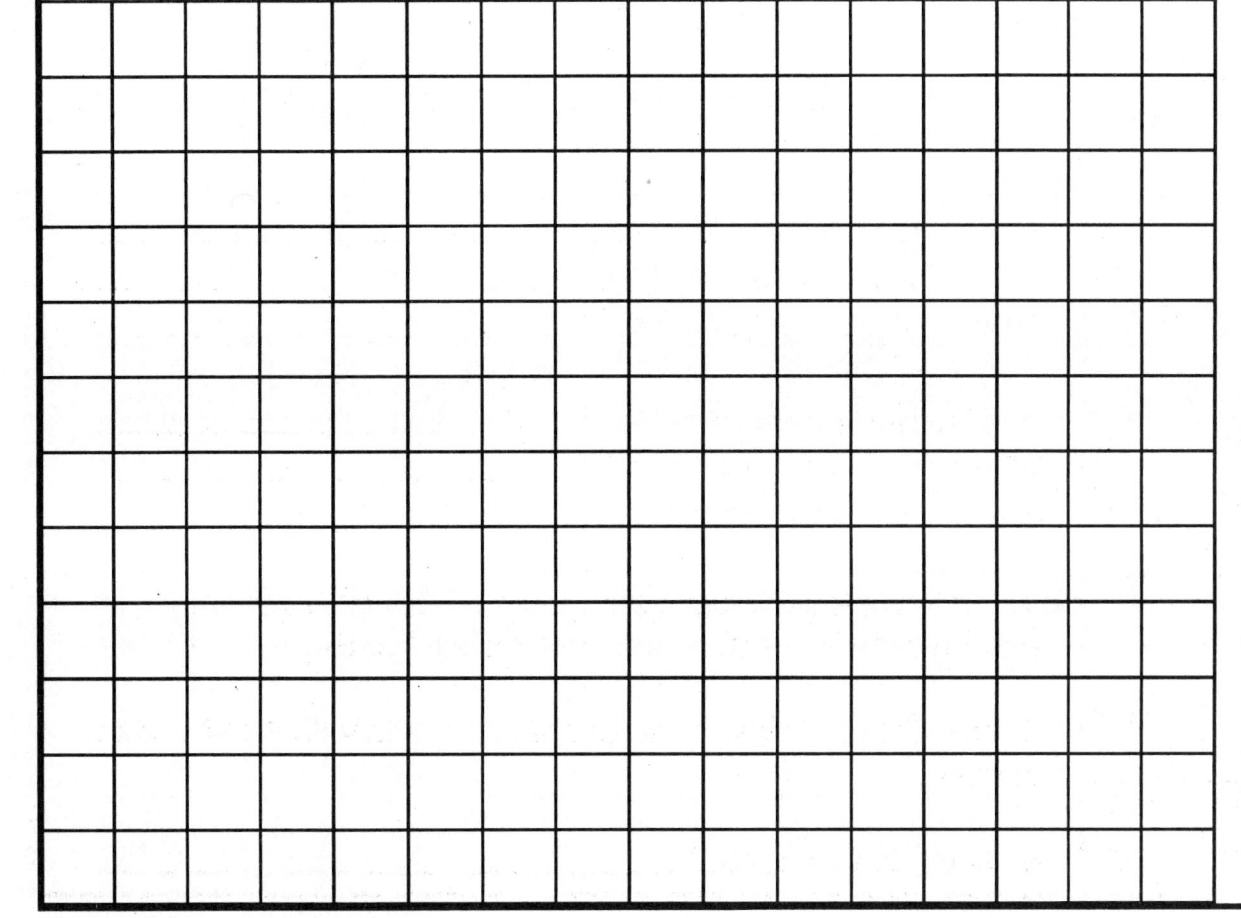

✤ Look carefully at the leaves, and then fill in your predictions:

- ☐ has the largest area.

- ☐ has the smallest area.

- ☐ and ☐ have the same area.

✤ Count the squares/parts of squares to find the approximate area of each leaf.
Write your answers under the labels.

✤ Were your predictions correct?

_____

Teacher Timesavers: Measurement skills

131

Area

Square centimetres

Square centimetres

You will need: a pencil, a collection of small flat objects.

Each square on the grid below is one square centimetre (1cm²).

♣ Place some small objects on the grid.

♣ Draw round them and calculate their areas in square centimetres (cm²).

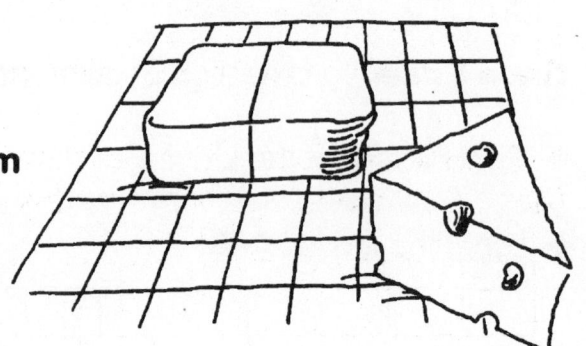

Name _____

Area
Find the area

Find the area

You will need: centimetre-squared paper, a pencil.

♣ Find the area of each of the following shapes. They are all made from 1cm squares.

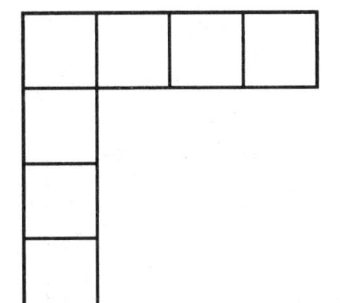

Area = _____ cm^2

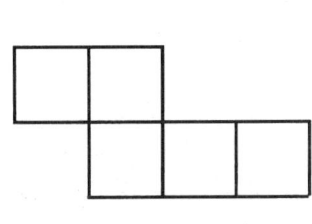

Area = _____ cm^2

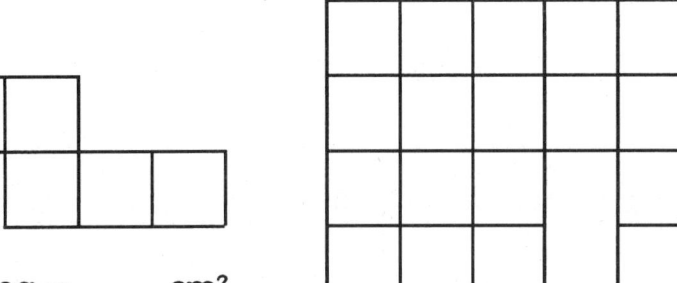

Area = _____ cm^2

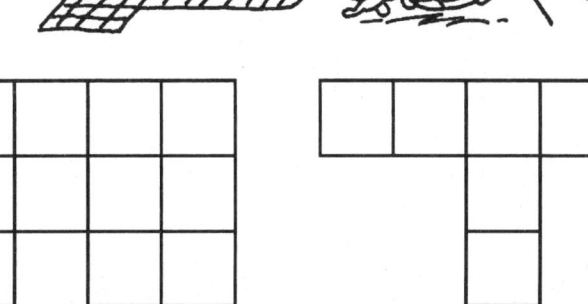

Area = _____ cm^2

♣ On centimetre-squared paper, draw as many different shapes as you can that cover an area of 12cm^2.

♣ Find the total area of this placemat.

Area = _____ cm^2

Teacher Timesavers: Measurement skills

Area

Square metres

Name _____

Square metres

You will need: a pencil, sticky tape, scissors, a metre ruler, paper.

✤ Using sticky tape and a metre ruler, mark out a square with 1m sides on the floor.

The area of the square is one square metre (1m²).

✤ How many people can stand on the square? _____

✤ How many chairs fit on to the square? _____

✤ Using large sheets of paper, make some squares with an area of 1m².

✤ Working in a group, use your squares to measure the surfaces in the table below.

✤ Write your predictions first.

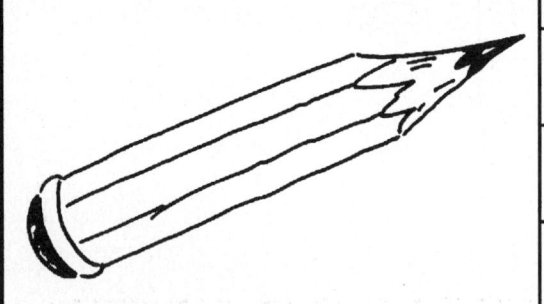

Surface	Prediction (m²)	Area (m²)
the classroom floor		
the corridor floor		
the cloakroom floor		

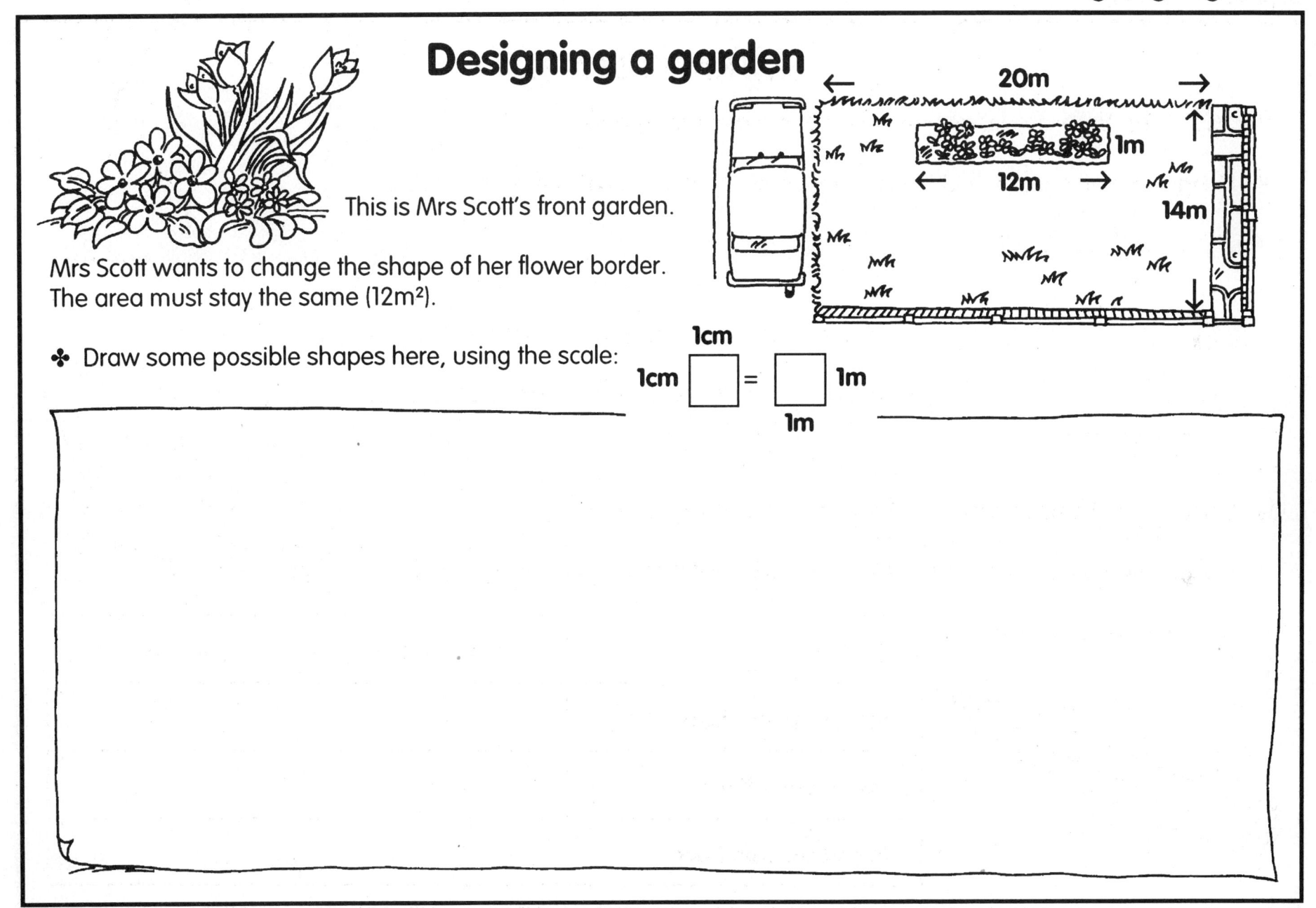

Name _____

Area

Designing a garden

Designing a garden

← 20m →

1m

← 12m →

14m

This is Mrs Scott's front garden.

Mrs Scott wants to change the shape of her flower border. The area must stay the same (12m²).

✤ Draw some possible shapes here, using the scale:

1cm × 1cm = 1m × 1m

Teacher Timesavers: Measurement skills

135

Area
Blackout!

Name _____

Blackout!

You will need: a metre ruler, a pencil.

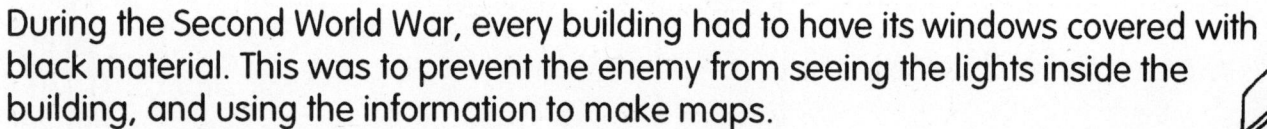

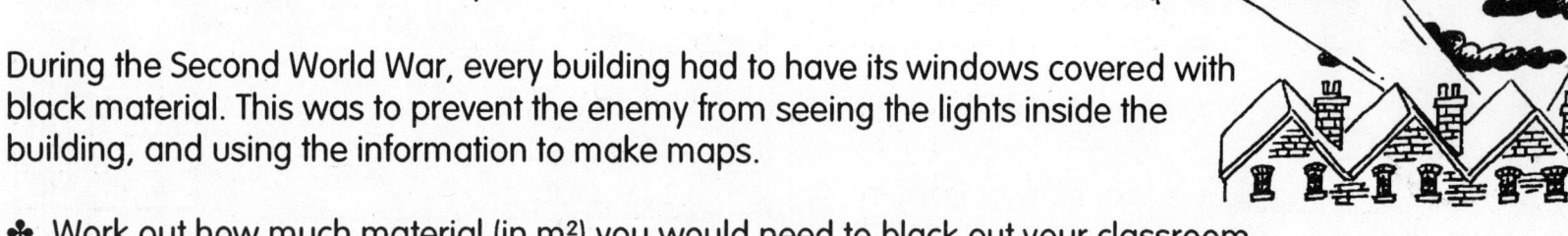

During the Second World War, every building had to have its windows covered with black material. This was to prevent the enemy from seeing the lights inside the building, and using the information to make maps.

♣ Work out how much material (in m²) you would need to black out your classroom.

♣ The material is 1.5m wide. How many metres will you need?

♣ The material costs £2.25 per metre. How much will it cost to black out the classroom?

Name _____

Area
Squares

Squares

♣ Fill in the information about each of the squares below.

Number of rows _____
Number of squares
in each row _____
Area in squares _____

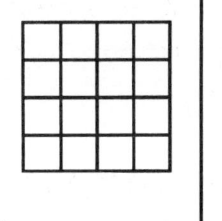

Number of rows _____
Number of squares
in each row _____
Area in squares _____

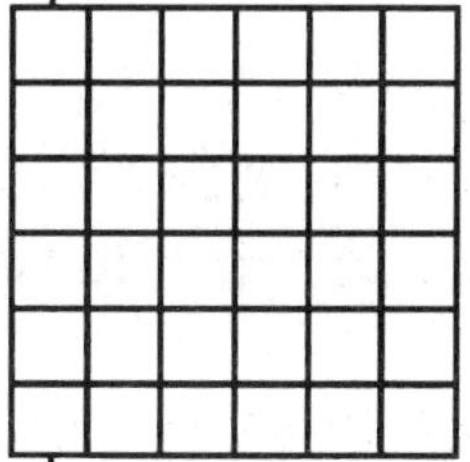

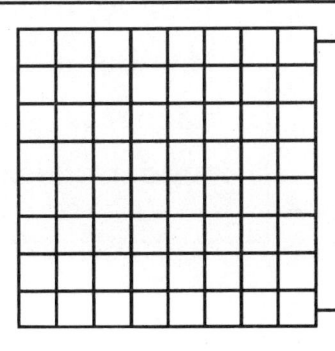

Number of rows _____
Number of squares
in each row _____
Area in squares _____

Number of rows _____
Number of squares
in each row _____
Area in squares _____

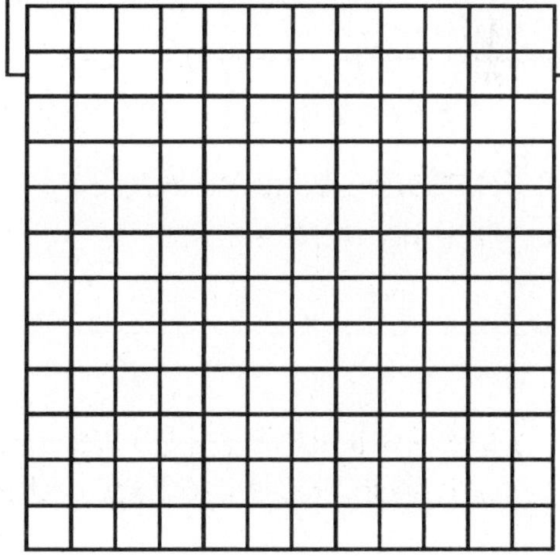

♣ Is there a quick way of calculating the area of a square? Explain your idea.

_____
_____
_____

♣ Using your idea, calculate the area of a 14cm square.

Area
Rectangles

Rectangles

✤ Fill in the information about each of the rectangles below.

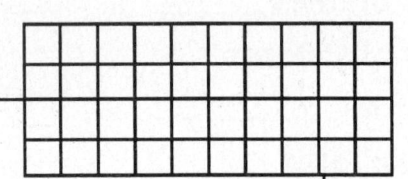

Number of rows _____
Number of squares in each row _____
Area in squares _____

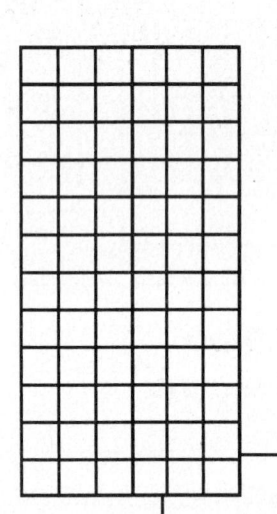

Number of rows _____
Number of squares in each row _____
Area in squares _____

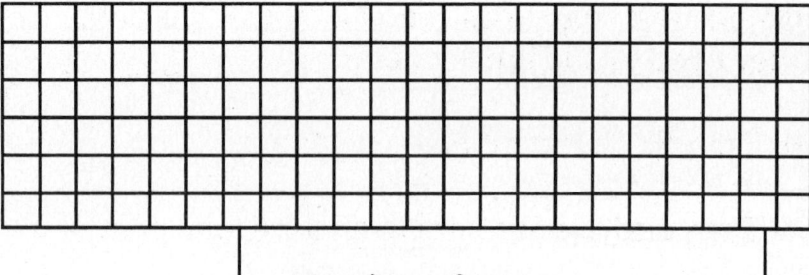

Number of rows _____
Number of squares in each row _____
Area in squares _____

✤ Is there a quick way of calculating the area of a rectangle? Explain your idea.

_____

_____

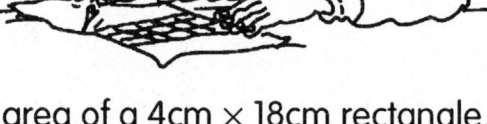

✤ Using your idea, calculate the area of a 4cm × 18cm rectangle.

Teacher Timesavers: Measurement skills

Name _____

Area

Gardens

Mr Akram, Mr Bourke, Mrs Kimptos and Mr Skipton are going to buy grass seed for all their gardens. They need to find the total area.

✤ Calculate the area of each garden.

✤ Then add the answers to give the total area of all the gardens.

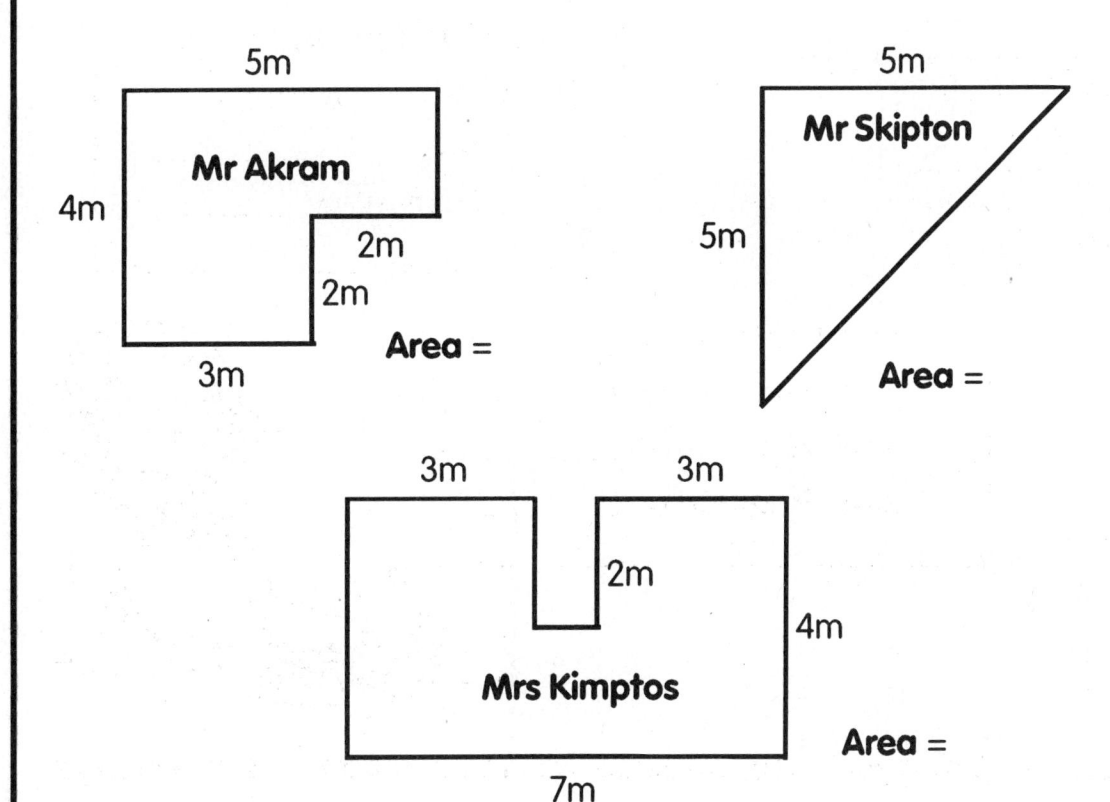

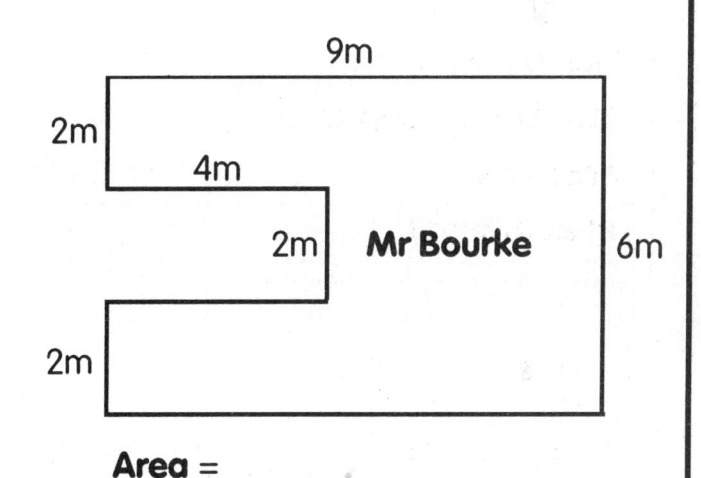

Mr Akram
5m, 4m, 2m, 2m, 3m

Area =

Mr Skipton
5m, 5m

Area =

Mr Bourke
9m, 2m, 4m, 2m, 2m, 6m

Area =

Mrs Kimptos
3m, 3m, 2m, 4m, 7m

Area =

Total area =

Teacher Timesavers: Measurement skills   139

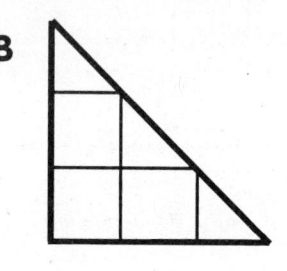

Area

Right-angled triangles

Name _____

Right-angled triangles

You will need: a centimetre ruler, a pencil.

♣ For each of the triangles on the right:

- Complete the square or rectangle around the triangle (triangle **A** has been done for you).
- Find the area of the square/rectangle and write your answer in the table.
- Find the area of the triangle and write your answer in the table.

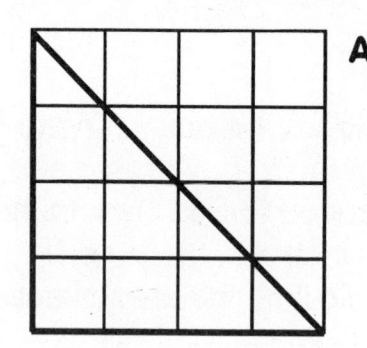

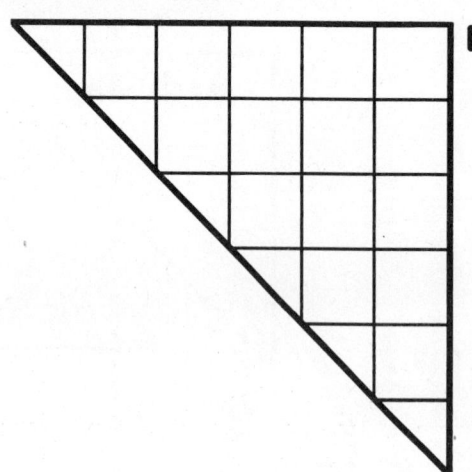

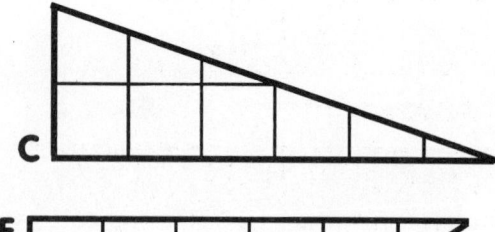

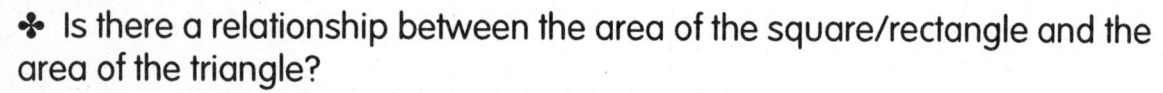

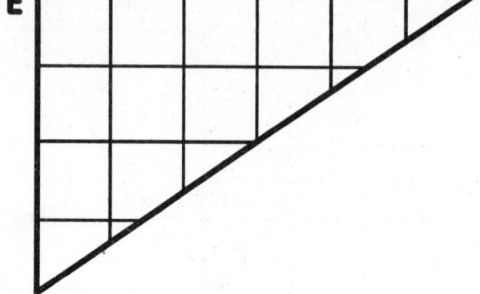

Triangle	Area of square/rectangle around it (cm²)	Area of triangle (cm²)
A		
B		
C		
D		
E		

♣ Is there a relationship between the area of the square/rectangle and the area of the triangle?

♣ Now complete this sentence:

The area of a right-angled triangle is _____ the area of the square/rectangle around it.

140

Teacher Timesavers: Measurement skills

Name _____

Area
One into two

One into two

You will need: a centimetre ruler, a pencil.

♣ Draw a line on each of the triangles to divide it into two right-angled triangles.
♣ Mark the right-angles (   ).
♣ Now find the area of each of the original triangles.

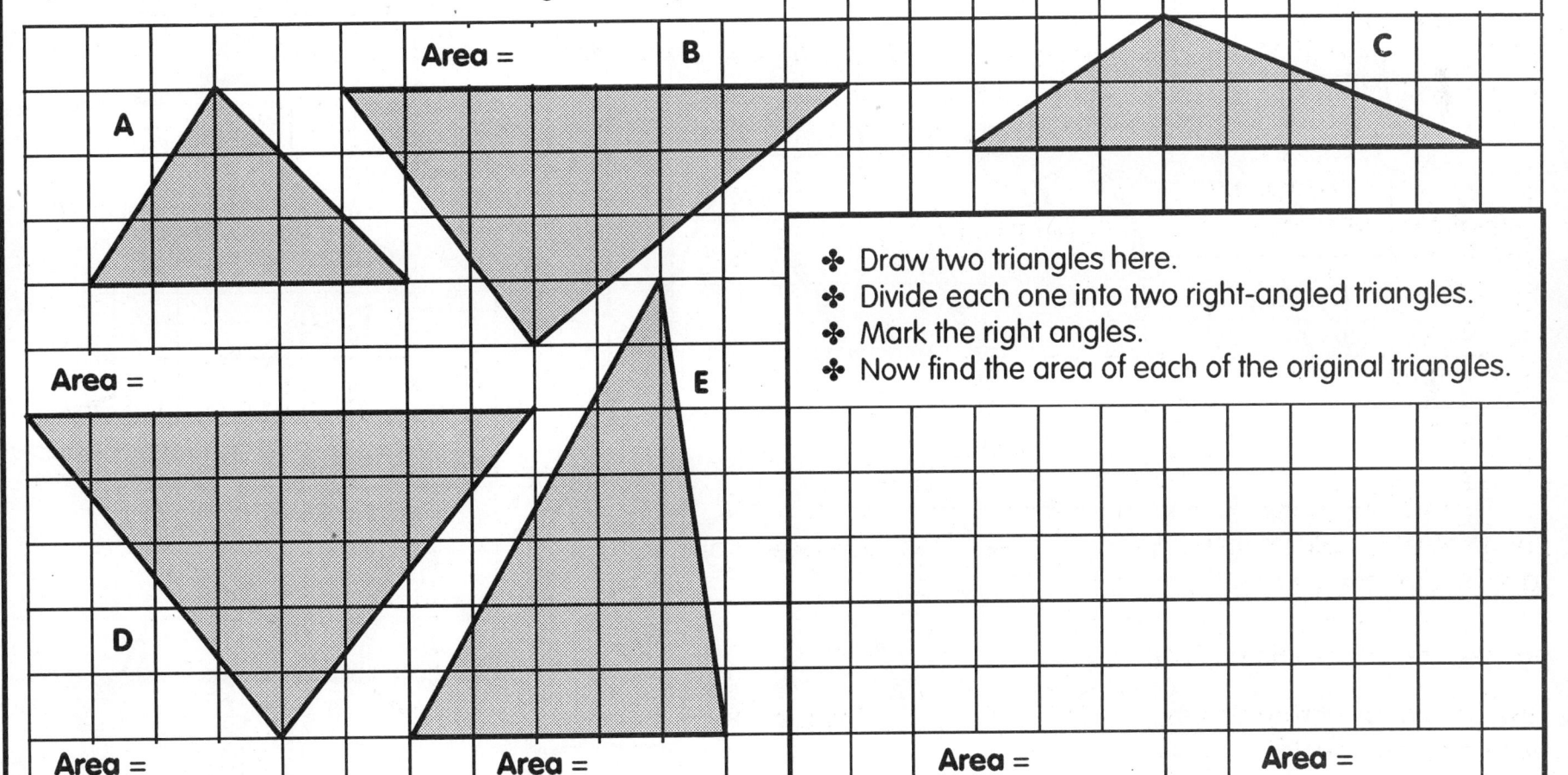

A

Area =   **B**

Area =   **C**

Area =

♣ Draw two triangles here.
♣ Divide each one into two right-angled triangles.
♣ Mark the right angles.
♣ Now find the area of each of the original triangles.

E

D

Area =

Area =   **Area =**   **Area =**   **Area =**

Teacher Timesavers: Measurement skills

Area
Kites

Kites

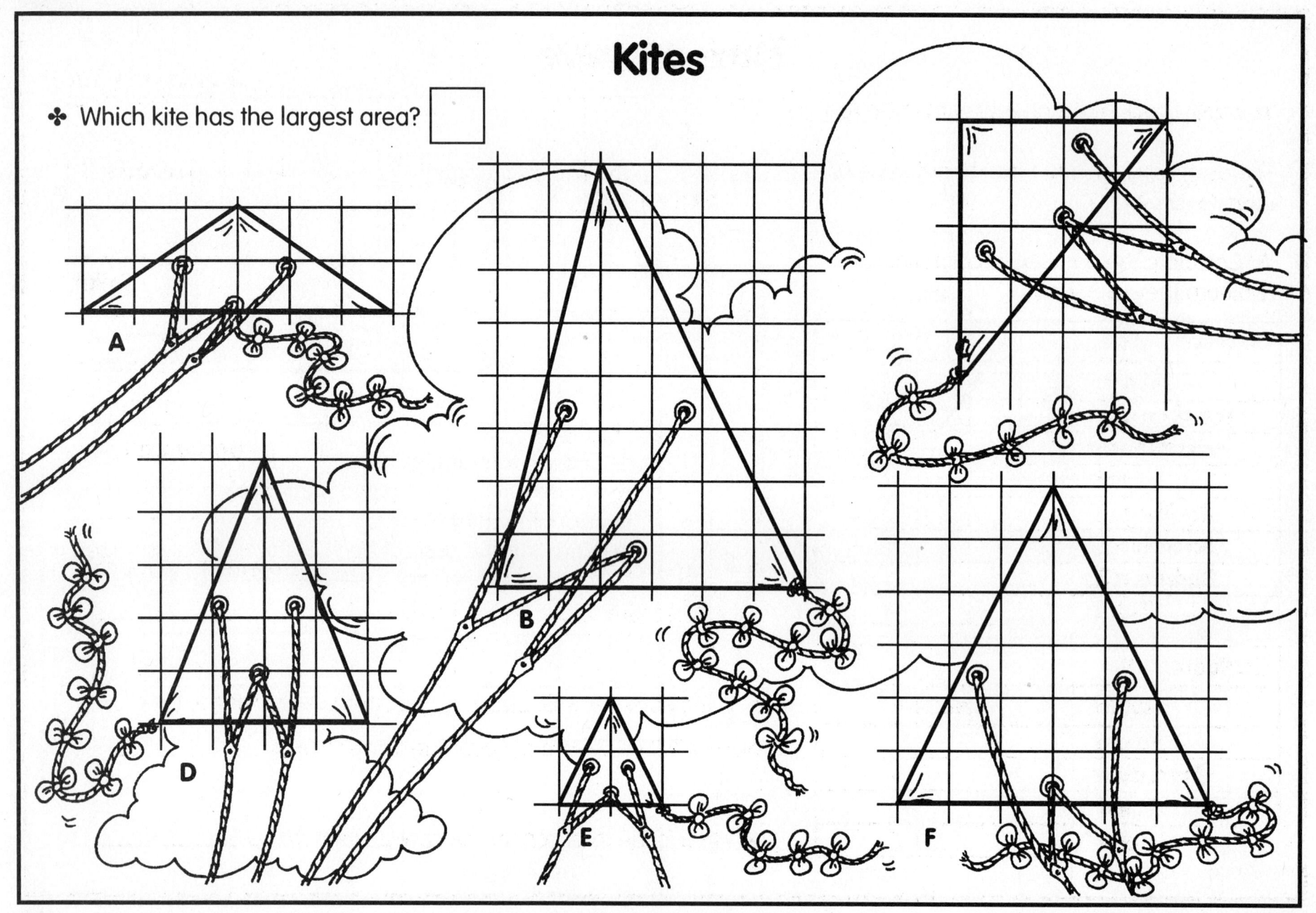

✤ Which kite has the largest area? ☐

A

B

D

E

F

142

Teacher Timesavers: Measurement skills

Name _____

Area
New carpets

New carpets

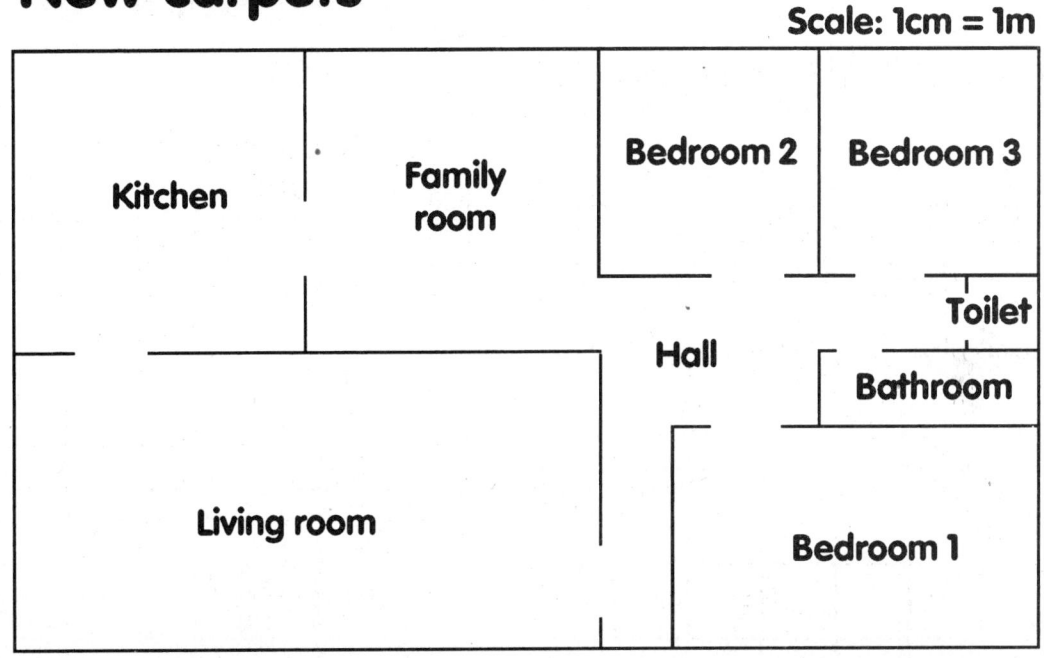

Scale: 1cm = 1m

You will need: a pencil, a centimetre ruler.

The owners of this flat want to put in new floor coverings.

♣ Calculate the amount of carpet and linoleum they require.

Carpet	
Room	Area(m²)
Family room	
Living room	
Hall	
Bedroom 1	
Bedroom 2	
Bedroom 3	
Total	

Linoleum	
Room	Area(m²)
Kitchen	
Bathroom	
Toilet	
Total	

♣ If carpet costs £ _____ per square metre, how much will it cost them to carpet the six rooms? _____

♣ If linoleum costs £ _____ per square metre, how much will it cost them to cover the three rooms? _____

♣ What is the total cost of the floor coverings? _____

Teacher Timesavers: Measurement skills

Area

Measuring farmland

Name _____

Measuring farmland

This is a map of a large farm in the north of Scotland.   Scale : 1cm² = 1km²

Key
- house/garden
- cattle grazing
- fishing lake
- forest
- land not suitable for use

♣ What is the total area of the farm? _____

♣ How much of the land is used for:

- the house/garden? _____
- cattle grazing? _____
- the fishing lake? _____
- forest? _____

♣ How much of the land is not suitable for use? _____

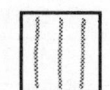

Teacher Timesavers: Measurement skills